The Good-For-You Marriage

The Good-for-You

MARRIAGE

How a Better Marriage Can Improve
Your Health, Prolong Your Life,
and Ensure Your Happiness

CLIFF ISAACSON AND MEG SCHNEIDER

Avon, Massachusetts

Published by
Adams Media, an F+W Publications Company
57 Littlefield Street, Avon, MA 02322. U.S.A.
www.adamsmedia.com

ISBN-10: 1-59869-476-6
ISBN-13: 978-1-59869-476-5

Printed in Canada

J I H G F E D C B A

Library of Congress Cataloging-in-Publication Data
is available from the publisher.

This publication is designed to provide accurate and authoritative information with regard to the subject matter covered. It is sold with the understanding that the publisher is not engaged in rendering legal, accounting, or other professional advice. If legal advice or other expert assistance is required, the services of a competent professional person should be sought.

—From a *Declaration of Principles* jointly adopted by a Committee of the American Bar Association and a Committee of Publishers and Associations

Many of the designations used by manufacturers and sellers to distinguish their product are claimed as trademarks. Where those designations appear in this book and Adams Media was aware of a trademark claim, the designations have been printed with initial capital letters.

This book is available at quantity discounts for bulk purchases.
For information, please call 1-800-289-0963.

To Kathy, my wife of 54 years—the adventure continues!

Cliff

· · · · · · · · · · · · · · · · ·

In loving memory of my husband, Bud—it was too short, but oh!, what a wonderful ride it was!

Meg

Contents

Acknowledgments

Cliff wishes to thank the thousands of couples who have sought his counsel and advice over the past four decades, and who, in the process, have taught him so much about what makes a marriage good and strong.

Meg wishes to thank her parents and her brother and sister-in-law, whose lasting marriages and healthy relationships have provided both example and inspiration.

Together, the authors also offer their thanks to their agent, Barb Doyen, whose enthusiasm and support are eclipsed only by her knowledge of the business, and their editor, Paula Munier, whose vision and good thinking made this book possible.

CHAPTER 1

Why Marriage is Good for You

A good marriage is good for you.

That isn't just a platitude. Mounting research shows that it is the literal truth. When your marriage is healthy, your body and mind are healthier:

1. **You live longer.** Two University of California–Los Angeles researchers, in a study published by the *Journal of Epidemiology and Health*, showed that married people really do have longer life expectancies than those who never marry. According to the study, your odds of dying prematurely if you've never been married are comparable to the odds of dying prematurely from high blood pressure or high cholesterol levels.

2. **You enjoy better mental health.** According to another recent study by Ohio State University researchers, depressed people actually reap more benefits from marriage than people who aren't depressed. This finding surprised even the researchers, who expected to see fewer benefits because depression in one partner can put great strains on a relationship. But it turns out that the emotional support and intimacy of marriage help ameliorate even serious depression.

3. **You're better off financially.** Research shows that married people tend to earn more and accumulate more wealth than their single or cohabiting counterparts.
4. **You're less likely to cheat or be cheated on.** Studies report that men and women who merely live together are four to eight times more likely to cheat on their partners than married men and women.
5. **You have more and better sex.** Married men and women report higher levels both of sexual activity and sexual satisfaction than their single or living-together counterparts.
6. **Your children do better.** Children of intact marriages are less likely to live in poverty, do better in school, put off having sex, live longer, and maintain closer, healthier relationships with their parents.

It might be hard to believe that a marriage license can confer so many benefits; after all, it's really just a piece of paper, isn't it? It's the relationship that matters, so couples in committed, long-term relationships should reap the same benefits even if they aren't technically married, right?

But they don't. According to Rutgers University Professor of Sociology David Popenoe, who also is co-director of the university's National Marriage Project, research shows that cohabitation—living with someone without the "piece of paper"—doesn't convey the same benefits in terms of physical health, emotional well-being, or financial security. This could be because people who are living together but not married may not be as focused on their partner's well-being as they are on their own. There is something about the public and legal nature of marriage—society's recognition of your union—that fosters better health in ways that merely living together doesn't.

We're going to explore all the ways a good marriage can be good for you. We'll show you what the latest research says and give you examples of how some couples have resolved issues that commonly crop up in a marriage. Occasionally, we'll provide tips for getting the most out of the information we have to share. And, at the end of each chapter, you'll find a "Honey Do List" of simple ways to enrich your relationship and your marriage. Our goal is not to offer a one-size "cure" for all the countless scenarios that can arise in your relationship, but rather to encourage you to use your new knowledge to find the solutions that work for you and make your good marriage as good for you as it can be.

Before we dive into all the research, though, let's take a look at some of the reasons that might have led you to get married in the first place. Most couples have several reasons for getting married, although they might not realize it at the time. No matter how long you've been married, it's wise to assess the reasons that brought you together to begin with and how they may have evolved over the course of your relationship. This kind of self-assessment can provide a basis for getting the most from your marriage in terms of physical, emotional and mental health.

What follows are eight of the most common reasons couples tie the knot. Sometimes they're good reasons; sometimes they're not so good. A lot depends on circumstance, point of view, and the needs or desires of each partner.

We're in Love

This is usually the first reason couples cite for getting married. After all, isn't that the whole point of the wedding ceremony? To join two loving hearts in the bonds of holy matrimony?

It depends on the nature of the love between you. When the feeling of love comes from a desire to do good for each other, it is the most forceful and compelling reason to marry. It means you are truly partners, each taking on the other's best interests as his or her own, willing and ready to set aside some of your self-interest for the greater good of your relationship together. When this is the nature of your love, the whole of your marriage becomes greater than the sum of each of you individually. And the real beauty of it is that, even though both of you make some sacrifices—you may not go out with your girlfriends on a moment's notice the way you did when you were single; or you may not go fishing as often as you did when you were single—it doesn't *feel* like an unreasonable sacrifice. Sure, you may heave a wistful sigh once in a while for the days when you could stay out until four in the morning without having anyone worrying about you at home, but that occasional nostalgia won't escalate into panic that you're somehow missing out on something by being married.

Sometimes, though, that isn't what we really mean when we say we love someone. Sometimes what we really mean is more akin to what we mean when we say, "I love that car," or "I love those shoes," or "I love that house." When *things* strike our fancy like that, we're motivated to *possess* them—not to take care of them, or look out for their best interests, or learn more about them. We want to *own* them. We want to be able to point to them and say, unequivocally, "This is *mine*."

We use the same kind of language quite often when we're talking about loving another person. Valentine's cards, poetry, and love songs urge the object of our affections to "say you'll be mine." Who hasn't said, jokingly or not, "Back off, girls (or guys)—(s)he's mine"? Of course, semantics alone doesn't signify that you want to own your partner rather than share your life with him or her. But it is worthwhile to examine whether that attitude goes beyond mere choice of words, and whether it has changed over time.

We'll Be Better Off Financially

This often is true, but sometimes it isn't. Studies show that married couples accumulate more wealth than single or cohabiting couples when they have joint finances and make money-related decisions together. However, if you keep finances separate—"his" money and "her" money—chances are you won't see any monetary gain from being married.

This isn't to say that spouses can't or shouldn't have their own pots of money for their own use. But keeping all the money separate can create friction in the relationship and financial problems for each of you, together and separately.

Look at it this way: Decisions like major purchases (a house, automobiles, etc.) and planning for the future (retirement savings, college for the children, etc.) affect both partners not just financially, but emotionally, too. And those emotional factors are more likely to be given their appropriate weight in the decision-making when couples merge their finances. It's like creating a joint venture, except the business in this case is the business of creating a sound economic base for the growth of your relationship.

Money, along with sex and raising children, is one of the top sources of conflict between couples, married or not. You and your partner may have different attitudes toward money; one of you may be a saver, the other may be a spender, and neither of you may understand the other's point of view. This issue is so critical that we devote an entire chapter to it later on. For now, think about what your financial arrangements might say about the level of trust between you and your partner.

. . . .

Married People Earn More

According to several studies, just being married increases your earning power. Some studies estimate that a married man earns as much as 40 percent more than his single counterpart—a wage differential equivalent to the difference between a high school diploma and a college degree.

All of Our Friends Are Married

On the surface, this sounds like a bad reason to get married. Can't you just hear your mother? "If all your friends jumped off a bridge, would you jump, too?" But it's true that social circles can exert a lot of influence on the decision to get married. It's hard to be the only single person when all your friends are married; you don't have the same kind of responsibilities, the same kind of attitude toward the future, and maybe not even the same kind of attitude toward the present. You cannot be single and married at the same time. This can be true even if you're living with your partner but not married. It's just not the same.

Religious upbringing and/or beliefs can be an adjunct to this kind of social pressure. If your faith expects you to get married (or if the faith of your family makes them pressure you to get married), that can be tough to resist. However, most religions encourage couples contemplating marriage to delve deeply into their reasons for wanting to marry; they don't generally promote marriage just for the sake of marriage.

Marriage Prevents Suicide

Studies show that married people have lower suicide rates than single people, a difference attributed to the often stronger social networks of friends and family married people have. Meaningful social relationships give us both a sense of personal value and a sense of responsibility toward others.

Again, the importance and effects of "fitting in" with your social circle may have changed over time. Maybe it wasn't a factor when you first got married—perhaps you were the first of your friends to tie the knot, for instance—but it may have become an important one as your social circle has grown to include more couples than singles. Conversely, a spate of breakups among your friends may exert its own kind of strange pressure on your marriage as you try to figure out what makes your relationship different or more lasting than theirs. Understanding how those pressures influence you, now and then, can give you more effective strategies for dealing with them.

We Want Security

The key issue here is what kind of security you seek. If security to you means a united front in the face of problems, that's a good thing. If it means knowing your partner has to be faithful now that you are married, you may be in for betrayal later on. And if it means securing the relationship with your partner, like tying down a boat in a storm, that could portend future troubles, too.

One couple who sought counseling fell into this latter definition of seeking security. They had been going together for about a month, and they wanted to get married. When pressed about their reasons for wanting to marry so quickly, the prominent desire that emerged was to preserve their relationship. After just a month, they were already having problems severe enough that they felt their relationship was falling apart. And their solution to these problems was to get married. Maybe they thought their problems would magically evaporate once they said their vows. Maybe they each thought the other would be more committed to resolving the problems after the marriage license was signed. Either way, they were kidding themselves.

. . . .

Marriage Lowers Rates of Violence

A landmark U.S. Justice Department report showed that single women were as much as five times more likely to be victims of violence than married women, and single men were four times more likely to be victims of violence than their married counterparts. It appears the security afforded by marriage is not just emotional, but physical.

Security is one of the great benefits of marriage. Partners provide strength, encouragement, and support for each other during tough times. When one spouse has reached the end of her rope, the other can shoulder the burden for a while. Knowing you have someone there you can count on for these things is a gift of inestimable value.

But you can't have each other's back if you're spending most of your time looking over your shoulder. A gold band and an official piece of paper don't provide security; you and your partner give it to each other.

We Can Support One Another

Like the security issue, support as a reason for getting married can be a double-edged sword. At its most beneficial, support is mutual and covers emotional issues, relationship issues, stress, and a whole bunch of other areas. If the support is one-way, though—if one partner carries most of the responsibility for providing emotional support for the other and gets little in return—that imbalance inevitably will create stress in the marriage. The supportive partner will get exhausted and very likely resentful, and the dependent partner will be disappointed when the level of support dips below what he or she has come to expect.

Of course, the giving and taking of support is not going to be a 50-50 proposition every minute of every day. If your spouse is laid off, for instance, you'll probably provide more support while the search is on for a new job, encouraging him or her to perhaps explore a different field, go back to school, or what have you. If you're battling a serious illness, your spouse will provide more support by giving you a strong shoulder to lean and sometimes cry on, perhaps by taking over some of the household responsibilities you have usually done, and so on. At any given time, the balance of support between you may be out of whack. Just as investment experts recommend taking a long-term view of the stock market, your perspective on marital support should take the long view. Over the years, in a well-balanced relationship, the amount of support you each give and receive should even out.

. . . .

Marriage Brings Better Mental Health

Several studies have shown that married people have lower rates of depression, schizophrenia, and other mental distress than single people. Married people also tend to manage stress and anxiety better than single people do, and they more often report feeling good about themselves and their lives—what psychologists call "global happiness," an overall sense of well-being.

Support is equally, if not more, important when times are good. A recent study published in *The Journal of Personality and Social Psychology* indicates that lukewarm reactions to things like promotions, awards, or other good happenings can do more damage to a couple's bond than hardship. Sharing each other's excitement, taking pride in each other's accomplishments, and otherwise celebrating the positive events in each other's lives provides an emotional boost that lasts long after the event itself is old news. On the other hand, consistently negative or even indifferent reactions to such events can be withering to a marriage.

Related to this is the sharing of burdens. Again, it's a good thing when it's a flexible arrangement that takes into account both the small and large blips that can turn your usual routine into hash. It's not so good when it's rigid, because those blips— and you *know* you can't avoid blips forever—will carry added stress when you aren't strong enough to bend. It can be as small as a meeting running late or as big as a car accident. If one spouse is always in charge of cooking dinner, for example, a late meeting for that spouse can throw the whole household's schedule out the window. If the other spouse is always responsible for taking out the trash and breaks his or her leg in an accident . . . well, you get the idea. The key to successfully supporting each other and sharing the burdens of everyday life is being able to roll with the punches.

We Want to Provide a Home for the Children

Children can be a great source of satisfaction for couples, and a great source of stress. And sometimes it's not so easy to separate the two. One of the key areas to explore is the expectations you and your partner have about parenting. How will you share the work? Who will take the child to doctor's appointments, daycare, after-school activities? Who will help the child with homework or problems with friends? How will you arrange time alone together, and how much of a priority will that be?

Those are what might be termed the practical aspects of parenting. There are philosophical aspects to consider as well. Do you and your spouse share the same views on discipline? What about religion? Education? General moral values? All of these areas can cause lots of unpleasantness if the two of you have widely differing opinions.

These same issues come up in blended families. If one or both of you have children from previous relationships, how will you handle raising those children? How will your relationships with your former partners affect what you do now?

It may seem like we're stating the obvious here, but honest dialogue on these topics is absolutely critical to successfully navigating the child-rearing obstacle course. Too often, couples just assume they share the same ideas and expectations, and when difficulties crop up, they are taken by surprise.

. . . .

Children Fare Better in Intact Marriages

Study after study has shown that children raised by single parents, and even those raised by someone other than both parents (a grandparent, for example), are at significantly higher risk of living in poverty, being victims of child abuse, dropping out of school, using drugs, and becoming sexually active at a young age. On the other hand, grown children of intact marriages live longer and report closer relationships with both parents.

We'll Have More Time Together

Like being in love, wanting to spend time together can be a good thing or a bad thing, depending on why you want more time with your mate. Is it so you can keep tabs on each other, or so you can share mutual interests and hobbies? Is one partner or the other devoting every waking hour to your togetherness, at the expense of work, children, education, his or her own hobbies? Is this what you expect from your partner, or what your partner expects from you?

Healthy relationships require a certain amount of time apart. Everyone needs "me" time. It might be time to hang out with your friends, without your spouse. It might be time to pursue a hobby your spouse isn't interested in. Maybe you just would like a couple of hours to yourself to read a book, watch a favorite movie, or take a walk. As your life fills up with various obligations—work, children, social engagements, volunteerism or community involvement—"me" time automatically shrinks and sometimes disappears altogether. That, in turn, increases feelings of stress, exhaustion, even resentment toward the calls on your limited time.

Healthy relationships also require a certain amount of "us" time. Without it, one or the other of you is likely to feel neglected, taken for granted, or even unloved. "Us" time is, or should be, a continuation of the dating you did at the beginning of your relationship. Going out for dinner, taking a walk together, even chores like raking the yard or cleaning out the garage—all these and countless other activities give you a chance to interact with each other one-on-one, even learn something about each other. You cannot bond with another person without "us" time. And you cannot sustain that bond over a lifetime without building "us" and "me" time into your routine.

How much "me" and "us" time is enough? There's no one answer, because there's no one model for a marriage or for life. To help figure out the right balance for you, pay attention to how you feel. If you feel tired, stressed, drained of energy, that could be a sign that you're neglecting "me" time. If you feel like you don't know what your spouse is doing, thinking, dreaming, or feeling, then you probably could benefit from more "us" time. Remember, too, that just because you feel this way doesn't mean your spouse will have the same feeling or the same perception. It might take real effort to communicate your own feelings and needs to your partner in a way that he or she will understand.

We're Great in Bed Together

Sex is a powerful motivator for bringing two people together. Some people feel they can enjoy sex more after marriage, and, indeed, research indicates this is true: Married people tend to have more and better sex than single or cohabiting people. When sex is a mutual expression of love—and when it arises out of other expressions of affection—it is a beautiful and fulfilling experience.

But.

Sex can also be one of the most common areas of conflict for couples. If one partner is feeling stressed, tired, or unappreciated, sexual overtures from the other partner can be unwelcome. And if the other partner feels rejected, that can easily escalate into a whole crayon box of bad feelings whose colors seep inexorably into virtually every other aspect of your life together.

. . . .

Better Sex and Less Cheating

Various studies show that married people report having more active and more emotionally satisfying sex lives than their single counterparts, and married people are less likely to cheat on their spouses than couples who live together. One study indicates that cohabiting men are four times more likely to cheat than married men, while cohabiting women are eight times more likely to cheat.

Then, too, expectations about your sex life can cause problems. If you think sex three times a week is plenty, and your partner would like to have sex five or six times a week, at least one of you is probably going to be dissatisfied. Sexual tastes and affinities can be another area of conflict.

The good news is that most couples experience a boost in their satisfaction with their sex lives over time, perhaps because, as we age and become more emotionally intimate with our spouses, we are more comfortable expressing our feelings physically.

You can see now why it's important and worthwhile to examine the reasons that prompted you to get married, good and bad. Poor reasons don't necessarily doom a marriage to misery or failure, but understanding them might help shed some light on troublesome areas of your relationship. And the better reasons give you a chance to savor the joys in your marriage.

The Influence of Other Relationships

Other relationships can influence your relationship with your spouse, even if you aren't aware of it. Most of us know, for instance, that either partner can bring problems from previous romantic relationships into a marriage. But your relationship with your parents and how you experienced their marriage also can leave an imprint on your own marriage.

Self-Confidence

As children, we get different, though equally important, instructions on how to behave depending on which parent we're dealing with. Self-confidence—belief in oneself and the lessons for how to interact with others—comes from the parent of the same sex. Boys learn from their fathers how to interact with others as a man; girls learn from their mothers how to interact with others as a woman. Sons are less concerned about whether Dad loves them than they are about figuring out how to interact with Dad as a fellow male, and daughters are less concerned about whether Mom loves them than they are about figuring out how to interact with Mom as a fellow female.

In learning how to be men and women, children watch their same-sex parent for clues on how to act and how to treat others. These learned behaviors can indicate potential problems in the child's relationships as an adult. A daughter who sees Mom nagging Dad about money, household chores, or a myriad of other topics, for instance, may come to believe that nagging is the appropriate way to get a husband to do what you want. But if she sees Mom being sweet but persistent with a store manager, she'll learn that, outside the home, you use different tactics to get what you want.

Sons pick up similar cues from watching their fathers. A son who sees Dad swearing at Mom or calling her names in response to the nagging will infer that this is an appropriate response at home. If the son sees Dad supporting Mom in front of the store manager, though, he learns that this is what husbands do in public.

Self-Esteem

Your relationship with the opposite-sex parent can either complement or counteract the lessons learned from your same-sex parent. This is because self-esteem—our image of ourselves as being worthy of love, affection, admiration, and so on—comes from the parent of the opposite sex. While both parents can make a child feel loved and lovable, these messages carry the most weight in developing the child's self-image when they come from the opposite-sex parent. Thus a daughter takes to heart the way Dad treats her, while a son takes to heart the way Mom treats him.

Messages about appropriate behavior from the opposite-sex parent carry different emotional pointers than messages from the same-sex parent. If a daughter imitates her mother's behavior by nagging a brother and Mom reacts with disapproval or anger, the daughter will be confused; her mother nags Dad, the daughter reasons, so it should be OK for her to nag her brother—that's the way women are supposed to behave in the home. But if Dad reacts to the daughter's nagging with disapproval or anger, the emotional pointer from Dad's reaction is, "You are not lovable when you act this way." This can set up an internal conflict for the daughter: Mom acts this way, so this must be what women are supposed to do, but Dad doesn't like it, so he must not like Mom or me. The daughter's choice then becomes the irreconcilable one of being lovable *or* behaving the way women are supposed to; she cannot do both. As an adult, she is very likely to continue to play out this difficult role in her marriage—feeling unlovable when she nags and like she's neglecting her job as a wife when she doesn't.

One thing that can help if you find yourself in this must nag/can't nag trap is to ask yourself if it's OK for your spouse to be the way he or she is. Most of us would respond, "Yes, except for ..." and cite the trait or behavior that bothers us most—smoking, drinking, swearing, leaving dirty clothes on the floor, or whatever. The "except for" behavior is the top complaint; everything else is minor stuff you can deal with, even if it isn't your ideal. Identifying your top complaint moves you out of automatic nagging and into thinking about ways you can help your husband or wife stop the objectionable behavior or, perhaps, ways you can learn to live with it.

There's another parent-child dynamic that can influence your marriage without you necessarily being aware of it. If you had to struggle as a child to get love from your opposite-sex parent, that struggle likely will be reflected in your choice of a partner as an adult. It's a subconscious memory that tells you love can only be received when it is a struggle. A woman who had to fight for Dad's love is more likely to be attracted to much older men; men who are ten or more years older will represent the authority figure in her life, the same way Dad did when she was a little girl, allowing her to live out the lesson she learned in childhood of having to struggle to get love. Men who didn't feel loved by their mothers also are more likely to seek out significantly older women, for the same reasons. These kinds of marriages tend to be skewed more toward the dependency of the younger spouse rather than based on a partnership of equals. This doesn't mean these relationships are bad or certain to fail, but it might take more work—perhaps even professional counseling—to achieve a balance that feels good and is healthy for both of you.

Parental Issues

Good relationships with your same-sex parent indicate that your own marriage will be good, too. But problems with the same-sex parent in childhood can lead to serious issues in a marriage. One couple came to counseling because their arguments nearly always became physical; they would end up hitting each other. During their counseling sessions, they revealed that each of them had bad relationships with their same-sex parents; the wife didn't get along with her mother, and the husband didn't get along with his father. As children, each of them wanted to hit the parent they were having problems with, but of course they couldn't. Years later, they projected those frustrations and feelings of wanting to strike out on each other, with disastrous results.

Such issues aren't always so overt, of course. More often, there are triggers that recall the problem with the same-sex parent—innocent-sounding phrases, perhaps, like, "I don't like your hair short," or, "What did you do that for?" Because these triggers are often subconscious, the reaction to them can seem excessive and out of proportion, and that can set off an argument that neither of you saw coming. One tactic for heading off such arguments is to acknowledge your spouse's reaction— "You sound angry" or "You look sad"—followed by a request for more insight. Asking, "Why do you think you got angry when I said/did that?" helps your spouse step back from his or her emotions and think about the root causes of the reaction. Many times, just being able to identify the trigger diminishes its ability to do further damage.

Your Parents' Marriage

The relationship your parents have or had with each other also can have a powerful influence on your own marriage. You didn't merely witness their relationship; you experienced it. And its good and bad qualities likely will color, to some extent, your own experience as a grown-up in a marriage for many, many years.

If your parents' marriage was so difficult that you wished they would split up, you may find yourself thinking compulsively about divorce when problems arise in your own marriage. This could be so even if your parents remained married; the wish that one of them would make the move to escape the unpleasantness is subconscious, and it remains with you ever after. In essence, your memories from childhood tell you, "I will not do as my parents did. I will get out of this. I will get a divorce." The stronger and more compulsive this feeling is, the more likely it is that professional counseling is in order. If you feel this way but to a more minor degree, you might think about opening a dialogue with your spouse about your feelings of being trapped and wanting to run away (which is really what divorce is—an escape).

Of course, the best influence for your own marriage is if both of you come from happy, harmonious homes. People in these fortunate circumstances have learned from early childhood the patterns that enable them to relate to each other as adults. They can solve life's problems together without getting into hassles with each other.

That doesn't mean a less-than-idyllic childhood dooms your marriage to failure. It just means that you may have to work a little harder in some areas to make your marriage as fulfilling as you want it to be. And, as the research shows, that hard work is well worth the effort. In the following chapters, we'll explore in depth the reasons we've discussed for getting and staying married, and how to get the most from each of those reasons so you can keep your marriage, your partner, and yourself happy and healthy until death do you part. We start with one of the most common areas of conflict: your finances.

1. Celebrate the good things that happen in each other's lives, even if all you have time for is a congratulatory hug.
2. Find ways to build "we" and "me" time into your life together.
3. Identify the balance of work, running the house, and family responsibilities that feels fair to both of you, and do what you can to maintain the balance that works for you.

CHAPTER 2

Sharing the Wealth

Here's the good news: Married couples tend to earn more money than single people and are less likely than single, divorced, or widowed people to live in poverty, and, as you may guess, people who aren't poor tend to be healthier than those who are.

The bad news: Money is, if not number one, among the top three sources of conflict for couples, right up there with sex and raising children. It isn't just a sore point when finances are tight, either. Money—and the managing of it—stabs right to the core of our emotions, our dreams, our expectations, our sense of self-worth, and our ideas of right and wrong. It is so fundamental a part of us that, according to the American Psychological Association, it is the primary cause of stress for nearly three out of every four American adults. Yet it remains something we seldom talk about except in the most abstract terms; indeed, many of us have been raised to believe that it is impolite to bring any remotely personal financial topic into a conversation. Unfortunately, this attitude too often is carried into marriage, the one place where it is vital to have those conversations.

. . . .

Does Marriage Make You Feel Poorer?

Harvard University researcher Elizabeth H. Gorman reported that married couples tend to be less satisfied with their financial situation than those who have never been married. Divorced people fell somewhere in between the married and never-married in their level of financial satisfaction. Interestingly, husbands and wives were equally likely to be dissatisfied with their pay and overall financial picture, a finding Gorman attributed to the fiscal stresses of parenthood. It may be that married couples with children feel more money pressures because they have to plan not only for their own futures but for things like college.

Money challenges couples because handling money demands communication and cooperation in a way that nothing else does. You have to be able to articulate your own financial goals and desires to your spouse (which means you have to be able to articulate them to yourself), and your spouse has to be able to do the same; you have to identify the emotional responses each of you has to money, or the lack of it; you have to figure out the logistics of "your," "my," and "our" money that works for your relationship. Most critical, you and your spouse have to be able to trust each other. And nowhere does a lack of trust show up more clearly than in dealing with finances.

Any number of factors can influence how you feel about and react to money matters, ranging from the wiring of the human brain to the attitudes your parents had toward money to your own personality traits. The more you know about these influences, the better prepared you will be when you and your spouse start talking seriously about how, when, and why to spend money.

The Pleasure and Pain of Spending

For years, the conventional wisdom among economists and others who study spending habits was that the act of purchasing is a rational process based on factors like price, perceived value, need, and competing needs. The theory went something like this: When one part of the brain starts egging us on to buy a new computer, another part steps in to argue that the current computer works fine, and besides, we should save the money for the kids' college fund or for next summer's vacation or for the new tires we know we'll need soon for the car. If the pro-computer part of the brain can come up with compelling arguments for making the purchase—if there's a killer sale on now, for instance—we buy. If those arguments aren't strong enough to overpower the college-vacation-tires part of the brain, we don't buy.

Recently, though, researchers have found that the rational model is wrong. In fact, according to experiments conducted by a team of behavioral economists from Carnegie Mellon University and a team of psychologists from Stanford University, our emotions have their say in the purchasing decision long before the rational parts of our brain begin collecting their arguments for and against.

Using magnetic resonance imaging (MRI) scans, the researchers found that the region of the brain associated with pleasure, called the nucleus accumbens, became active when subjects saw something they wanted to buy. The insula, the region that fires up when you experience or expect something unpleasant, was activated when the subjects saw the price associated with an object they could buy. Conclusion: We are hard-wired to experience pleasure when we see something we want and to experience pain when it comes to parting with money.

And yet we continue to spend. According to several consumer financial groups, the average American carries $7,000 in credit card debt alone. That doesn't even take into account the high interest rates often associated with credit cards, or the other indebtedness many Americans have like mortgages, home equity loans, auto loans, and personal and student loans. And when you consider that, according to the U.S. Census Bureau, the median American household income is around $46,326, it becomes pretty clear that a lot of us are living well beyond our means.

How can this be so, if we really are hard-wired to feel pain when we spend money? The Carnegie-Stanford researchers think the answer may lie in the way we spend in the twenty-first century. Using cash tends to provoke the pain response, but credit apparently doesn't, at least not until the bill arrives. Because we don't feel the pain immediately, it's easier to overspend when we whip out the credit cards. The same may hold true for other kinds of debt, too; as long as the monthly payments don't trigger our pain threshold, we may purchase more expensive houses or cars than we would if we had to peel hundred-dollar bills off the bankroll in our pockets.

The Miser in All of Us

According to recent research, just thinking about money makes humans less cooperative, less giving, and less connected to others. Psychologists from the University of Minnesota conducted a series of experiments in which some subjects were given subconscious cues to think about money and others were not. When the subjects were later asked to complete other tasks, the subjects who had been primed with thoughts about money were slower to ask for help, slower to offer help to others, and were less generous with their time and money when asked to give to a worthy cause. This was the first known study of its kind, so it's too soon to say whether this behavior carries over into marriage. But it's worth keeping in mind if you or your spouse—or both of you—tend to withdraw when it's time to talk about your finances.

The research also may indicate why some people are tight-wads. It isn't necessarily just an undesirable personality trait; there might be a physical cause for cheapness. Tightwads might have an overly sensitive insula or an underfunctioning nucleus accumbens, either of which may prevent such a person from spending, even when the spending is in his own best interest. One couple, for example, argued over whether to purchase four new tires for the car or replace only the two that were in the worst condition. The husband, a self-described tightwad, wanted to go with the less expensive option, while the wife contended that it made better sense to replace all four tires now, especially because winter was fast approaching. The husband finally agreed, but it was a genuine struggle for him to do so. Only when the wife raised the safety issue was he able to overcome his deep aversion to spending money, and even then he was unable to feel good about it. Rather, he viewed it as an unavoidable unpleasantness.

Attitudes Toward Money

The stereotype of couples' attitudes toward money is that husbands earn it and wives spend it. In fact, men are just as likely to be spenders as women, and women are just as likely to be savers as men. However, it is not uncommon for spenders to marry savers, which adds another element of tension to the already stress-laced topic of money.

A good place to start defusing the tension is by examining your own and your spouse's attitudes toward money. Here are some questions to help you start the discussion. Keep in mind that these are only a starting point, and the only right answers are the ones that honestly describe your and your spouse's responses.

1. How do you feel when you have cash in your wallet?
2. How do you feel when you don't have any cash in your wallet?

3. How do you feel when you open bills?
4. How do you feel when you spend money?
5. How do you feel when you decide not to spend money?
6. When you balance the checkbook, do you round off or figure it out to the penny?
7. Which best describes your view of money?
    a. It's worthless until I buy something with it.
    b. It's a tool to help me achieve my current and long-term goals.
    c. It's a resource to be cultivated and protected.

You may have noticed that most of these questions start with "How do you feel?" That's because so much of our behavior with money is tied up in our emotions. Money can make us feel safe, loved, powerful, independent, content, and worthwhile; lack of it can make us feel nervous, unloved, powerless, dependent, unhappy, and worthless. If you don't understand how your emotions are affected by money, it's hard to figure out an arrangement for handling the money that you and your spouse can both be comfortable with.

The sixth question provides a hint to your money-handling personality. People who balance their checkbooks to the penny tend to be more detail-oriented. They need to know exactly how much money they have on hand, and they tend to make detailed budgets that include not just monthly expenses but less regular ones like annual insurance premiums or quarterly water bills. People who round off tend to live more in the present and spend less time thinking about or planning for the future, figuring things will work themselves out. Again, it's not uncommon for these two types to marry each other, and these differing approaches can raise stress levels for each spouse.

The last question is based on information that educator and author Ruby Payne has used to identify class differences in attitudes toward money. Poor people tend to see money as a commodity that isn't worth anything until it is spent. People in the middle class see it as something to be managed so they can achieve their goals, such as buying a house, paying for the kids' college, or financing their retirement. Rich people see it as something to be invested so it will produce more money. The circumstances in which you were raised likely have the greatest influence on how you respond to this question, because these attitudes tend to be passed down from parents to children.

. . . .

Tips for Dealing with Debt

If you believe most financial advisers, credit cards are evil. They make it far too easy to overspend (by taking away the immediate pain response); the cost of using them is astronomical when you figure in interest, various fees, and potential penalties; and, if you pay only the minimum every month, it's virtually impossible to rid yourself of any significant debt. So how do you avoid the credit card trap? First, don't beat yourself up if you've racked up a big balance. Instead, direct that energy to reasserting control over your spending. If it's too easy for you to reach for the plastic, take it out of your wallet and keep it in a drawer at home. Pay as much as you can toward the balance every month. Finally, call your credit card company and ask for a lower interest rate. You might even be able to get them to waive late fees or overlimit charges if you call and explain your situation.

Money as Control

The hand that rocks the cradle may rule the world, but the hand that writes the checks tends to rule the roost. In fact, controlling the household finances is a common way of controlling a spouse.

Men and women both do it. They might do it in different ways and perhaps from different motives, and they might not even be aware of the more far-reaching effects of their financial control.

One man who came in for counseling had controlled the household finances for the entire 35 years of his marriage. He had never involved his wife in handling the money that came into the house; he never even shared information with her about their financial situation, and he certainly never gave her independent access to their money. He told her how much she could spend for groceries and the like. He paid the bills. He approved or vetoed additional expenses.

He didn't want her to work outside the home because, he said, it was his job "to provide for the family." In fact, it was another way to keep his wife from having any money of her own. When, finally, she received an inheritance that he could not control, she left him. She had wanted to leave the marriage for some time, but this was the first time in 35 years that she had the financial resources to do so. In counseling, the man realized that his iron grip on the family finances was really an attempt to keep his wife from leaving him.

This particular manifestation of a lack of trust isn't unusual, especially among people who suffer from commitment phobia. Commitment phobia makes a person feel trapped in a relationship, so he (or she, although men more commonly exhibit signs of commitment phobia) devises ways to avoid becoming close to his wife. He may reject her efforts at giving him affection or attention, for instance, by not returning a hug or refusing to be drawn into conversation.

On some level, though, the commitment-phobic person realizes that his behavior is pushing his wife away, and the fear of being trapped battles with the fear of being abandoned. He doesn't want to be close to her, but he doesn't want her to leave him, either. So he searches for ways to make it difficult for her to leave. One way is to control the money: If she doesn't have any money, she can't afford to leave him.

This strategy sometimes is used even in marriages where both spouses earn paychecks and even when husband and wife have their own accounts. Typically, the household money isn't pooled into a joint account, so each spouse is responsible for some of the household bills. The spouse with commitment phobia then will push more bills onto the other, thus ensuring that the other doesn't have enough money left over to enjoy any freedom—especially not the freedom to leave.

Another way to control money—and therefore your spouse—is to have a one-sided budget, where one spouse, usually the wife, creates the budget, moves the money into and out of savings and checking accounts, and pays the bills. When the husband suggests buying something, the wife's response often is, "We can't afford it." If the husband objects, she reinforces her position of monetary control by saying, "I'm the one who makes out the checks. I'm the one who knows where the money goes. I'm the one who knows what we can and cannot afford."

Sometimes control of the finances isn't actively sought but is passively ceded by one spouse to the other. There are several possible reasons for this: The ceding spouse may feel inadequate in dealing with money; he or she may not want the responsibility of managing the family finances; or, because so many of us have a hard time talking about money, the ceding spouse may just be unable or unwilling to negotiate a more equitable arrangement. The result can be disastrous for the relationship.

For example, one man counseled by Cliff had laid aside money for major house repairs. When it came time to do the repairs, he discovered that his wife had spent the money on other things—and unnecessary things at that. He was upset, but nothing changed;

his wife did the same thing again with an insurance check for hail damage, spending it on other things instead of using it to fix the damage. The breakdown in communication and cooperation was so complete that this couple eventually parted ways.

Money and Gender Roles

Even in the so-called "classless" American society, money has always been tied to our ideas of worth, including our self-worth. The less money we make, the less valuable we tend to feel. Men in particular are susceptible to this feeling, in part because of the traditional male role of being the provider for the family.

As more women earn higher salaries, the issue of who brings in more money can add to the natural stresses of dealing with finances. In addition to the fact that we tend to equate money with power, some men might feel less masculine if they earn less than their wives do, while women who earn more than their husbands might feel less feminine. Other, more subtle issues of insecurity might also arise. One spouse might fear on some level that there's no reason except money for the other spouse to stay in the marriage; this kind of insecurity might compel the higher-earning spouse to become a workaholic or the lesser-earning spouse to skid into depression.

One way to mitigate this additional stress is to recognize that money is only one form of contribution to the household. Cooking, cleaning, laundry, taking out the trash, yard work, and maintenance all have to be done, too, to make the home run smoothly, and those tasks are just as valuable as income. It's important that, whatever form it takes, each spouse feels valued for his or her contribution. It's also important that each spouse feels the burdens of running the house are shared fairly. Otherwise, you lay the groundwork for a whole series of arguments about who does what and what it's worth.

. . . .

More Wives Move into Breadwinner's Circle

According to the U.S. Census Bureau, in households where couples are married and both earn paychecks, slightly more than a quarter of wives bring home more than their husbands. That figure is expected to grow as more women than men earn college degrees and choose higher-paying careers. Fortunately, according to a 2005 Gallup poll, younger adults are more accepting of the concept of role reversal—men as the primary homemakers and women as the primary wage-earners—so traditional gender roles may not cause as much friction in marriages in the future.

Negotiating as Partners

Any arrangement that gives monetary control to one spouse or the other, for whatever reason, is likely to cause trouble in the marriage sooner or later because it inherently places people who should be equals in unequal positions. While there is no universal "right way" to organize your financial life together, there are some basic tenets you can follow to build an arrangement that works for both of you and promotes communication and cooperation.

Talk about your dreams and goals. Do you want to buy your first home, or a larger home? Remodel or expand your current home? Start your own business someday? Retire early? Switch to a lower-paying but more rewarding career field? A good way to start this conversation is to ask, "What would you do if you won a million dollars in the lottery?" Knowing what you'd do if money were no object can help you identify the things you really want to do, even if you have to work harder for them. This also helps you distinguish between things you need and things you want. You might want a 1966 Mustang, for example, but what you really need is a reliable car to get you back and forth to work.

Prioritize your goals. Maybe buying that first house is less important to you than starting your own business. Maybe your spouse would rather invest money in your current home than look for another one. It's critical that you do this together, because you and your spouse might have different priorities; if you don't talk about them, it's easy to make false assumptions that will cause problems later on.

Create a budget together. Start with household expenses—mortgage, car payment, loan and credit card payments, utility bills, newspaper subscriptions, and insurance. Add in what you spend on groceries, gas, haircuts, prescriptions, and so on. Figure out whether there's any money left over when these expenses are covered, and then discuss how to use the leftover money.

If there isn't any money left over, talk about ways to trim your expenses. Some things you probably won't be able to cut, like your car payment. But you might be able to save money by switching grocery stores or using coupons, by carpooling or using mass transit, and so on.

If there is leftover money and you and your spouse disagree on how it should be used, explore compromises together. Say you have an extra five hundred dollars a month. You might want to use it for things like eating out or other forms of entertainment; your spouse might want to save it for the bathroom remodel you've been talking about or for another major purchase. Maybe you can agree to limit your monthly entertainment expenses to one hundred and fifty dollars and put the rest in savings for the long-term purchase.

Build some freedom for each of you into your budget. One common way to do this is to give each other regular "allowances"—spending money that can be used at each spouse's own discretion. Another way is to establish individual bank accounts, separate from the joint household account, so that each partner has control of his or her own pool of money.

Commit to the budget. A monetary plan only works as well as you and your spouse follow it. If either of you have trouble sticking to the budget, talk about it as soon as possible; maybe you need to tweak the budget to make it work. But you can't make adjustments if you don't know what's causing the problem, and the problem will only get worse the longer you ignore it.

Commit to each other. Think of your marriage as a joint business venture, with each other as the founding partners. Your financial fortunes depend on each other, so it is in your best interest to look out for your partner's best interest and vice versa. In this respect, it doesn't matter whether one spouse earns more than the other; each of you is taking a financial risk, and each of you has a responsibility to the other.

What Your Money Habits Say about Your Marriage

The strength of a marriage, like the strength of a body, can only be discovered when challenged. The most telling challenge to a marriage is the handling of money. And that makes the handling of money one of the most objective ways to evaluate the health of a marriage. The use of money in a marriage cannot be ignored or hidden (at least not for long), nor will misuse of money fix itself spontaneously. Money brings out both the best and the worst in us, and if a couple cannot find the proper balance in the handling of money, odds are that other elements of the relationship are out of balance, too.

If one spouse does the budgeting alone, that spouse likely is relied on to carry most of the total load in the marriage. If one spouse is passive about finances, that spouse probably is passive in the rest of marriage. If one spouse makes rules about finances, that person probably makes other rules for the marriage and family. If one spouse overspends, that one probably also is careless with time, crowds out available space with things and over-extends the various family resources. If one spouse controls the finances, that one probably also controls the other's time, behavior, and things.

By the same token, the use of money can show strengths and improvements in a marriage. When financial issues are resolved, other issues probably will be resolved, too, or at least eased. Couples who aren't in accord over their finances have a hard time enjoying each other because money troubles tend to obliterate each spouse's sense of humor and ability to relax; they can't connect emotionally. But couples who achieve harmony over their finances are free to be playful with each other and to find joy, love, and comfort in each other's company.

Honey Do List

1. Identify all the ways each of you contributes to the household.
2. Find ways to show that you value each other's contributions, even if it's just making a habit of saying "please" and "thank you."
3. Discuss and acknowledge each other's emotional responses to and attitudes toward money.

4. Work out priorities together by talking about your needs, goals, and dreams.
5. Negotiate a budget together and help each other stick to it.
6. Build trust in each other by being cooperative and honest in your discussions and handling of money.

CHAPTER 3

Keeping Your Sanity

Despite all the half-joking complaints that our spouses drive us crazy, the truth is that they help keep us sane. Various studies show that married people have significantly lower rates of depression and schizophrenia than single people, that married people are better at handling stress and anxiety and are more motivated to hang in there during difficult times than single people, and that married people have higher "global happiness" levels than single people.

So, yes, your husband's habit of leaving exactly four-tenths of an ounce of milk in the carton so he can put it back in the refrigerator and claim it wasn't empty might drive you to distraction, and your wife's tendency to leap to answer the phone as if she were expecting to be told she's the next Publisher's Clearinghouse million-dollar winner might make you want to scream. But underneath it all, the bond you share is promoting better mental health for each of you.

Mutual Reality Checks

The conventional definition of sanity covers "soundness of mind," "soundness of judgment," and general "mental health." But there's another dimension to sanity, and that is being in touch with reality. Without getting too philosophical about the nature of reality and how we decide what is real and what isn't, let's just say that reality has many viewpoints, and yours might not coincide with someone else's. Because we don't automatically consider reality from any viewpoint but our own, we can easily get out of touch with what might be described as the "whole" reality. Our spouses, whose viewpoints are different from ours, can help us get back in touch—if we pay attention.

. . . .

Optimism Pays

The naturally optimistic tend to have healthier hearts and cardiovascular systems than people who are naturally pessimistic, according to a study in the Netherlands that was published in *The Archives of General Psychiatry*. The jury is still out on whether the Eeyores among us can improve their physical health by changing their mental outlook, but another study, this one reported in *The Journal of Personality and Social Psychology*, indicates that couples enjoy longer, more satisfying relationships even if just one of the pair is an optimist. Optimists tend to view their partners as supportive, and that seems to improve a couple's ability to resolve conflicts constructively, the researchers said.

Of course, we can't pay attention if we aren't communicating, and lack of communication is one of the most common problems in any relationship. Sometimes we miss information. Sometimes we miss meaning. And the lack can be on either the giving or receiving end.

I Told You . . .

Communicating information is simply relating facts, like what time the alarm is set for or where the car keys are. When you have to repeat facts or repeatedly ask for facts, there's a problem: Either the information wasn't conveyed clearly, or the listening was turned off. Both of these problems stem from childhood experience.

If you were like most children, you probably were trained not to talk. Adults around you told you, "Keep quiet," and, "Don't interrupt." Maybe they shushed you; maybe they told you that children "are to be seen, not heard." You learned to hold your tongue, even if there was something you really wanted to say, until the time was right and you were allowed to speak. Sometimes the right time never came, and you never got a chance to say what you wanted to.

As an adult, you still wait to say what you want to say. You don't interrupt, even when it would be appropriate. You keep waiting for the right time, and, as a result, you may have to rush to get your say in, or you may never get to say anything at all. Sometimes you may even think you told your partner something when, in fact, you never got around to it.

Problems on the listening end also are rooted in training we got as children. Lectures from parents, teachers, or other adults—whether they were corrective or just plain boring—triggered our desire to get away, and, since we couldn't get away physically, we learned to get away mentally. "Blah, blah, blah," the adult would say, and we learned to nod at the appropriate times, when all the while we were thinking about what we were going to do after school or wondering what it is that makes grass green. If the adults caught us not paying attention, they'd order us to listen, and we had to get cleverer about hiding our inattention.

The problem is we got so good at it that, by the time we grew up, we were doing it almost automatically. Whenever someone starts talking at us instead of to us, our bodies go into smile-and-nod mode while our minds step out for a quick trip to Jamaica. And, sometimes (gasp!), we even do it with our spouses.

You and your spouse can't help each other stay in touch with reality if you can't keep each other informed. Both of you have to be free to talk as well as to listen. Otherwise, information doesn't get shared, and then both of you are cut off from each other's input. Here are some tips to make sure each of you is getting the information you need:

- **Let go of the frustration.** Recognize that each of you may be contributing to your lack of communication. Consider the possibility that you didn't say what you thought you did or didn't listen to what your spouse told you.
- **Use nonjudgmental language to clarify things.** "Did I tell you about the electric bill?" or "I know you said something about the electric bill, but I can't remember what it was" is an easy way to get over momentary lapses in information-sharing.
- **Decide to speak.** Making a conscious decision to say what you want when you're ready to say it can overcome the keep-quiet training you got in childhood.
- **Decide to listen, for the same reason.** If you find your attention wandering, acknowledge it and ask your partner to repeat what he or she was saying.
- **Make a conversation date.** If there are just too many distractions at the moment, ask for a rain check. "I'll tell you about it when I get home" or a similar phrase is a simple way to agree to set aside time to share information.

You Don't Understand . . .

Communication between couples often breaks down not at the information level but at the level of meaning. This is the "why"—the purpose or significance—behind the facts. "Why did you set the alarm for 5 A.M. instead of 6?" "I have a breakfast meeting at 7. I thought I told you about that." "You're right; I had forgotten." When your partner asks you "why," he or she is probing for the meaning behind what you said or did.

But sometimes we don't ask why. Instead, we assign our own meaning to our spouse's words or actions. As a result, we interpret those words or actions to be unreasonable, even crazy. They don't make sense to us with the meaning we've concocted.

This is another bad habit we were trained for in childhood. Who doesn't remember an impatient parent's stern rebuke: "Do you understand?!"? We didn't understand, but we didn't dare say so. We just meekly indicated we understood and hoped that later on we would figure out what it was we were supposed to understand. As adults, then, we feel compelled to understand even when we don't have enough information; this is why we jump to conclusions. We decide on the meaning before we get a full explanation (or even any explanation), and we are immediately ready to agree or, more often, disagree with what we perceive the meaning to be.

The thing is, we aren't all that good at explaining, either. Care to guess why? Yes, childhood training. As soon as a parent or other authority figured demanded, "Why did you do this?" we had only two courses open to us: self-defense ("It was his idea!") or ignorance ("I don't know"). Neither one worked very well, and both usually led to a lecture (during which we were not allowed to speak, so we let our minds wander), followed by "Do you understand?!" Really, it's a wonder we're able to communicate at all.

· ·

You're Not the Boss of Me

Husbands really do ignore their wives, especially when wives ask them to do something, new research shows. A husband-and-wife team at Duke University determined that "reactance"—the urge to do the opposite of what your spouse or boss asks—occurs at a subconscious level. Subjects were asked to name someone they saw as controlling their lives and someone who wanted them to have fun; then they were asked to solve jumbled word puzzles while the names of the people they selected were flashed subliminally. Not surprisingly, the subjects performed better when they were cued with the name of the person who wanted them to have fun.

As adults, it's not uncommon for us to freeze up when someone asks us why we did or said something. We can't use self-defense; it makes us sound like we're making excuses. We can't claim ignorance; if they didn't buy it when we were seven, they're not going to buy it when we're forty-seven. And if we haven't overcome our keep-quiet training, we're not inclined to answer anyway.

But we cannot expect others to understand us if we aren't willing or able to explain ourselves. Explaining is how we convey the meaning behind the facts. It requires us to take our time, get our thoughts organized, and pay attention to make sure the other person is getting the meaning we intend to convey. If the other person isn't getting it, it requires going back and finding other ways to explain what we mean.

Couples often complain of not understanding each other or not being understood. You can see now that there's a real basis for that complaint. If you find that communication of meaning is breaking down in your relationship, there are steps you can take to repair it:

- **Decide to wait for a full explanation.** This stops you from jumping to conclusions and making judgments based on insufficient information.
- **Decide to ask questions.** If the meaning you've interpreted doesn't make sense to you, asking "What do you mean?" will help fill in the blanks.
- **Get confirmation of your interpretation.** Phrases like, "You're worried about the bills," or "You don't want to go to your family reunion" invite your spouse to agree or disagree, which lets you know whether you understand.

- **Ask for confirmation of your explanation.** Verbal and nonverbal cues will give you an idea of whether your spouse understands your meaning, but it never hurts to double-check with a phrase like, "Do you see what I mean?"
- **Allow yourself time to figure out how best to convey your meaning, and do the same for your spouse.** "I don't know how to explain it" lets your spouse know that you aren't simply ignoring the issue; when your spouse says this, you can help him or her collect his or her thoughts by asking questions like, "Do you want to skip the reunion because you're feeling stressed from work?"

There is an almost infinite spectrum of possible meanings, and it may take time and effort to pinpoint the real meaning. It could involve expectations from others or expectations from yourself. It might involve emotions that go unrecognized or ignored. It may revolve around hope, fear, anticipation, anxiety, sadness, anger, loneliness, or a myriad of other feelings. Determining meaning is often complex, a process that continues over a lifetime. Fortunately, the basic tools are quite durable: "What do you mean?" is always a good question, and listening to the explanation is always a good response.

Couples Who Play Together Stay Together

Misunderstood humor often causes friction between husband and wife—and that's too bad, because humor that is understood, appreciated, and enjoyed not only indicates good communication, it's good for your health. A study by cardiologists at the University of Maryland Medical Center showed for the first time that laughter contributes to heart health; according to the research, people who have heart disease are less likely to laugh than people without heart disease. The exact mechanism remains unknown, but the prevalent theory is that laughter reduces stress, which is known to interfere with the protective lining of blood vessels and can lead to inflammation, plaque build-up, and other complications.

Remember the Time . . . ?

A study by a professor at Appalachian State University shows that just remembering times when you laughed with your partner can increase your satisfaction with your relationship. Reminiscing about fun times strengthens the bond between you and makes you feel closer to your spouse. This effect is strongest when you reminisce together, the study noted.

Humor is so often misunderstood partly because there are so many different kinds of humor. There is sarcasm, twisting the meaning of another's words: "You can look through my wallet anytime, honey." "Sure, now that there isn't any money in it." There's the April Fool's type of humor: "I asked for a raise like you told me to, and they fired me." There's teasing: "I am shocked— shocked, I say—that you would do such a thing." There's the put-down: "Nice purse. Did they have a sale at Bag-Ladies-R-Us?" And there's the insulting kind of humor that seems to imply the target is lazy or stupid: "You can remember a meal you had fifteen years ago, but you can't remember to take the trash out on Thursdays?"

Not Funny!

Misunderstood humor can be a big source of stress, and the misunderstanding can quickly escalate into a full-blown argument. If you don't get the humor, sarcasm can offend you, "April

Fooling" can feel mean-spirited, teasing comes across as criticism, put-downs feel genuine, and insults seem serious. Meanwhile, your partner, who has been trying to play with you, feels bad because you didn't understand the humor and rejected because you didn't respond in your own playful fashion.

There are lots of things that can make attempts at humor fall flat. We might not be paying full attention to the cues that tell us it's humor; we might be under unusual stress; we might just be in a bad mood and not open to laughing about anything at the moment. Sometimes the humor isn't communicated properly, but, at least half the time, the problem is with the receiver. And, as with other types of communication, the obstacles to sharing and enjoying humor were constructed in childhood when we were told to quit playing and do our chores. The message we carry with us into adulthood is that work and play are mutually exclusive, so we tend to squash our playful side and concentrate on the serious work of being a grown-up.

Returning the Serve

Humor is like Ping-Pong: You have to return the ball for the game to be any fun. The nice thing about humor is that you don't have to return the same kind you receive. Sarcasm can be answered with teasing, insults can be answered with sarcasm, and so on. The key to sharing humor—and the stress relief that comes with it—is the sharing.

Raising the amount of humor in your relationship can be a challenge because so much of our resistance to humor is rooted in the subconscious. Sometimes, just knowing it's OK to use humor lets you lighten up and give your playful side a chance to express itself. Sometimes, you might need to give yourself a little internal encouragement. Try telling yourself, "Turn on the part of me that knows how to play." Getting away from home can make it easier to indulge in and enjoy humor, because the quit-playing training from childhood took place largely at home. And if you still don't quite know how to return the humor that's served up to you, you can just smile or laugh to let your partner know that you've received the joke and recognized it as humor.

One other thing to keep in mind: Humor is a very good measure of compatibility and intelligence. Two people who don't get each other's sense of humor likely won't last as a couple; in fact, they usually won't even be attracted enough to each other to become a couple. It requires similar levels of intelligence—not education, but intelligence—to understand and appreciate another's humor, too. It doesn't matter whether one of you holds a doctorate and the other is a high-school drop-out; if you can share humor, you're on the same plane of brain power.

Speaking of Brain Power . . .

One of the ways married couples keep each other healthy is by encouraging healthy habits (see Chapter 10 for more on this). Now scientists are starting to figure out why habits like regular exercise affect things like memory loss and other brain functions.

According to a report in the *Proceedings of the National Academy of Sciences*, exercise improves brain function by promoting the creation of new brain cells. The growth, tracked by MRI scans, occurs in a region of the hippocampus that is associated with age-related declines in memory—something that shows up in most of us at around 30 years old. The next step, the researchers said, is to determine whether specific exercise regimens are more effective than others in promoting cell growth in this area of the brain.

Worry Makes Things Worse

Psychologists familiar with "math anxiety"—the feeling of dread many students experience before a big test—say worrying about how well you'll perform on the test makes matters worse by draining the brain's relatively limited working capacity. The brain needs this space to do complex tasks like solving difficult math problems, and if that space is full of anxiety, it can't solve the problem. This same mechanism may be at work when we're confronted with any kind of complex problem; anxiety literally prevents us from coming up with solutions or making decisions. If you find yourself (or your spouse) paralyzed by worrying, you might try the Scarlett O'Hara method of getting a handle on things: Think about it tomorrow. Making the decision to defer worrying frees you to concentrate on the things that need your attention.

Meanwhile, other researchers are looking into connections between mental stress and physical injury. Sports psychologists are finding that there's a direct link between an athlete's emotional health and the likelihood of getting injured, and the American College of Sports Medicine has alerted coaches, trainers, and team doctors of the increasing evidence of such connections. Stress can cause you to overlook potential dangers on the field, for example, and it can increase tension in your muscles, which in turn can result in sprains or tears. Even if you aren't an Iron Man athlete, stress can depress your immune system and make you more vulnerable to whatever virus is making the rounds at the office these days.

Let's Hear Some Feedback

The relationship between you and your spouse is like the relationship between the thermostat and the furnace. The thermostat gives the furnace information—feedback—so the furnace knows what to do. If the thermostat says it's too hot, the furnace shuts down for a while. If the thermostat says it's too cold, the furnace kicks on.

Similarly, we continually exchange feedback with our spouses, letting each other know in countless ways whether we're running too hot or too cold. This feedback is essential for us to get along, and, in fact, we seek such feedback from many sources. But because our spouses live with us day after day and tend to know us better than anyone else, they give us the most valuable feedback.

Feedback comes in several forms. We get an emotional reaction when we irritate or annoy, for example. Our spouses might become judgmental when we act in uncaring ways. Criticism can be a sign of carelessness on our part. Our spouses might get pushy if they feel we aren't facing up to difficulties, or they might get forceful if they feel we're being too passive. The form of the feedback can be a clue to the interpretation of the behavior that prompted it.

The Johari Window

One great tool for feedback is the Johari Window, developed in the mid-1950s by Joseph Luft and Harry Ingham. There are four panes in the Johari Window, representing what you and others know about you (the "open" pane), what you know about yourself that others don't know (the "hidden" pane), what others know about you that you don't (the "blind spot" pane), and what neither you nor others know about you (the "unknown" pane). From the list below, select five or six adjectives that you believe describe you; then have your spouse choose the same number of adjectives to describe you from the same list. Words that you both selected go in the "open" pane; words that you selected but your spouse did not go in the "hidden" pane; and words that your spouse selected that you did not go in the "blind spot" pane. The "unknown" pane represents the opportunity for each of you to gain new insights into your personality.

- Able
- Accepting
- Adaptable
- Assertive
- Bold
- Brave
- Calm
- Caring
- Cheerful
- Clever
- Complex
- Confident
- Dependable
- Dignified
- Energetic
- Extroverted
- Friendly
- Giving
- Happy
- Helpful
- Idealistic
- Independent
- Ingenious
- Intelligent
- Introverted
- Kind
- Knowledgeable
- Logical
- Loving
- Mature
- Modest
- Nervous
- Observant
- Organized
- Patient
- Powerful
- Proud
- Quiet
- Reflective
- Relaxed
- Religious
- Responsive
- Searching
- Self-conscious
- Sensible
- Sentimental
- Shy
- Silly
- Spontaneous
- Sympathetic
- Tense
- Trustworthy
- Warm
- Wise
- Witty

As we noted earlier, misunderstanding the meaning of communication is the quickest way to build a mountain out of a molehill. It's hard not to get defensive when our spouse is challenging our behavior or misinterpreting our meaning. But it's important, for the health of your relationship, to be able to understand the message without punishing the messenger. Fortunately, the standby "What do you mean?" not only gives you time to process what just happened between you and your spouse, it also forces you to take a step back and look more objectively at your own behavior. Then you can take corrective steps, like explaining that you're peeved at your boss, not your spouse, and apologizing for letting your frustration come out the way it did.

Not all the feedback you get—or give, for that matter—will be on the money, but as long as both of you are able to give each other feedback, you can help keep each other sane and in touch with reality.

Honey Do List

1. Laugh together.
2. Encourage each other to turn on the parts of you that know how to play.
3. Act as mirrors for each other, providing feedback in your mutual reflections.
4. Encourage better communication by acknowledging each other's nonverbal cues: "You look tired," "You sound frustrated," etc.
5. Unlock each other's problem-solving potential by giving each other permission to put off worrying.

CHAPTER 4

Goodbye, Lonelyheartsville

Several years ago, Wayne State University professor Steven Stack published his findings from a cross-national study of the correlation between marriage and loneliness. He found that, in sixteen of the seventeen countries sampled, married people are less lonely than single people, even when single people are living with their romantic partners; that both men and women reported being less lonely when they were married; and that loneliness was lower among married people even after the physical and financial benefits of marriage were adjusted for.

More recently, researchers have linked loneliness to physical ailments like hardening of the arteries and dementia among the elderly. One study found that persistently lonely older people had twice as much risk of developing symptoms of dementia, similar to Alzheimer's. That study's author theorized that loneliness causes depression, which in turn can limit the body's ability to compensate for age-related deterioration in neural pathways.

Of course, we all feel lonely sometimes, whether we're married or single. But, given the physical and mental health benefits of being socially and emotionally connected to others, it's worthwhile to explore ways to minimize those lonely times.

How Am I Lonely?

There's a difference between being alone and being lonely, and you can be one without necessarily being the other. But there are different kinds of loneliness, too. There's the restless, bored feeling we get when we've gone too long without interaction with other people; that's social loneliness, and it generally leads us to call up friends or family and invite them to lunch or a movie. If friends and family aren't available, we might go out to a bar, or go shopping, or log into an Internet chat room. What we need with this kind of loneliness is simple human contact, even if it isn't intimate or lasting. We just want a reminder that we aren't the last person on earth.

The other type of loneliness isn't so easily fixed. It's the chilly, isolated, depressing feeling we get when we suspect no one would miss us if we were to vanish without a trace. With this kind of loneliness, we can be surrounded by people and still not feel connected; in fact, we may even prefer to be alone when we feel like this, because the company of others only highlights how emotionally lonely we are.

Even though married people are less prone to these types of isolation, husbands and wives are still vulnerable to both social and emotional loneliness. An occasional bout of either kind is to be expected as a normal condition of life. Persistent feelings of loneliness of either kind can lead to other issues and areas of conflict in your marriage. First, though, it helps to know how you and your spouse feel about being by yourself.

Leave Me Alone (or Please Don't)

Different people feel differently about spending time by themselves, and you and your spouse probably have differing ideas about what it means to be alone. Understanding each other's attitudes toward solitude can help you avoid misunderstandings about each other's motives.

The natural loner

This person not only doesn't mind being by himself, he actually needs some time alone in order to function properly. If he can't get some alone time any other way, he may get up early or stay up after the rest of the family has gone to bed. His desire to be alone isn't a reflection of his feelings toward his family or friends; it's more like self-maintenance to keep himself balanced. Because this is such an elemental need for him, he'll be surprised if anyone is offended or hurt by it, and he'll have a hard time understanding people who don't have a similar need.

The follower

Even when this person would prefer to be alone, she won't say so for fear of offending you. She'll agree to whatever you suggest, rarely if ever offering her own suggestion. You might pick up on other cues that she's unhappy, tired, or otherwise not really into socializing, but she will be very reluctant to voice her own opinions or make her own needs known. She might even suppress her desire to be alone because she feels guilty about excluding you. If you're a natural loner, she'll probably interpret your need for time alone as an indication that you're upset with her, and she'll feel guilty about that, too.

The over-booked

This person is constantly torn between what others need from him and what he needs for himself, and when he can't do it all for everybody, he feels that he is somehow inadequate. If he does take time for himself, he tends to view it as a weakness, an imperfection. More often, this person will push himself to the brink in meeting others' needs and neglect his own, and he will do this until he collapses with exhaustion. In extreme cases, the only time he spends on himself is when he's too sick to do anything else. Ironically, he tends to be very understanding of others' need for time alone and will do whatever he can, even taking on extra work or responsibilities, to help meet that need.

The life of the party

The most sociable of all social animals, this person rarely is alone, and, when she is, it's usually because she's overwhelmed by the demands placed on her. These spells don't last long, though, because she gets bored if she's by herself for too long. She is the most likely type to strike up a conversation with a stranger wherever she may be; she is equally comfortable chatting with an old school friend or talking with the clerk at the grocery store. She seldom understands others' need for solitude and may feel hurt if you need time away from her.

The reluctant joiner

This person may spend a lot of time alone, but it isn't because he wants to; it's because he isn't convinced that other people want him around. At work, he might require cajoling to join the group for lunch. At home, you might have to tell him specifically that you want to sit with him on the couch and watch TV. When he does prefer to be alone, it's usually to work through a grouch, and if he is forced to be sociable in those circumstances, he likely will be sullen and unpleasant. Since being alone equals being unwanted to him, he doesn't understand why someone would choose to be alone and may assume that you're grouchy if you require time to yourself.

The Socially Lonely Spouse

Social loneliness occurs in marriage when circumstances keep you from spending time together. Things like business travel, civic meetings, or running the kids to soccer practice or orthodontist appointments might keep you physically separated for most of the day, the week, or even the month. If both of you have equally full calendars, chances are you will miss each other without necessarily feeling lonely. But if one of you is off on a business trip and the other has free time to fill, the one with the free time is probably going to look for ways to fill up that time.

In most instances, this won't cause any problems for your marriage. But sometimes the tactics we use to help us get through one tough time become a habit, and sometimes habits become destructive. Some women whose husbands travel a lot fill up the empty hours with shopping, for example. There's nothing wrong with taking a trip to the mall while your husband is at a Saturday conference. But if the shopping becomes compulsive—if you buy things you don't need with money that should be put toward bills or the vacation fund or the children's college savings—it will cause problems in your relationship. In a typical scenario, your husband will get angry about your spending, and you'll blame him for leaving you alone so often.

Similar problems can crop up when the wife is gone too much. The husband might spend his evenings hanging out with his friends at the corner pub—again, nothing to raise concern when it's an occasional thing, but something that could easily become destructive if engaged in too frequently. And, again, the underlying problem of one spouse being lonely can all too quickly escalate into a whole menu of other problems.

. . . .

Stay in the Same Bedroom

Experts recommend couples strive to sleep in the same room, even if snoring or other nighttime issues arise, because, for many of us, the few minutes in bed before we fall asleep at night is our only chance to have an uninterrupted conversation. There are several strategies for dealing with snoring, cover-stealing, and other stresses of sharing a bed. But there is no substitute for being in the same place at the same time to protect each other against social loneliness.

At its worst, social loneliness can become self-perpetuating, because we might not be inclined to change our patterns even when the catalyst that started the pattern—the absence of our spouse—is no longer present. This is one reason why lifetime dating is so important. (See Chapter 6 for dating tips and strategies.) Making the commitment to "date night" helps you stay focused on your relationship even in the midst of all the other demands on your time. It also helps keep the socially lonely spouse from becoming emotionally lonely because dating reinforces your bond.

The Emotionally Lonely Spouse

Emotional loneliness can be devastating, especially in marriage. This happens when the bond between you is neglected; without continual maintenance, it will wither away until you no longer feel connected and united. This kind of isolation flows from persistent feelings of being taken for granted, misunderstood, unappreciated, and unvalued. At its worst, emotional loneliness can lead us away from the marriage, into affairs or divorce; at best, it makes us feel like strangers in our own homes.

Certainly, every couple has times when they feel like they're standing on opposite sides of a canyon, each unable to understand the other's point of view and unable to make themselves understood. Most of the time, we find ways to heal the breach so we can stand together again. Temporary divisions should not be viewed with excessive alarm. But a lingering sense of "drifting apart" should raise some flags: It's a good indication that you need to work on stabilizing your bond.

What causes couples to drift apart? Sometimes it's as simple as forgetting to make spending time together a priority. You can't keep up on what's going on in each other's daily life if you never have time to talk to each other. And if you don't feel like your spouse knows, much less understands, what you're dealing with at work or at home, there's a good chance you don't feel like you're compatriots, standing shoulder to shoulder to face the world. In fact, you may come to view your spouse as more of an acquaintance than a partner. Sometimes it might even feel like a chore to explain what's been going on in your life, especially if it has been a while since you've discussed anything more involved than whether there's enough toilet paper to last until the weekend.

Another thing that can make you lose touch with each other is failure to resolve your conflicts. Time pressures can contribute to this; sometimes it's just easier and more convenient to drop a difficult subject. But ignoring problems doesn't make them go away, and building up resentments fosters a tendency toward separateness. It makes sense, really. If your spouse doesn't understand how you feel and you don't have time to explain it, your inclination is to hide how you feel so you can avoid a time-consuming argument. Hiding feelings is the polar opposite of emotional intimacy, and you cannot sustain a meaningful bond with your spouse without emotional intimacy. It's a cycle that feeds on itself, and the longer it is allowed to continue, the harder it is to break.

Again, committing to lifetime dating can prevent the cycle of emotional loneliness from starting. Dating keeps you in touch with each other and with what's happening in your lives. Discussing the day's or week's happenings is a natural way to demonstrate interest in each other and share how you feel about things—ingredients that are as essential to maintaining a healthy bond as sunlight and water are to a healthy garden.

. . . .

Gender Differences in Loneliness

Men and women both are susceptible to feeling lonely, but not necessarily in the same ways. Women tend to be better at emotional intimacy because they're more comfortable sharing their feelings. But they may experience more social loneliness because they may feel less confident of how others will receive them; they may avoid situations where they would be required to initiate a conversation, for example. Men, on the other hand, tend not to be as comfortable with emotional intimacy, so may feel more emotionally lonely than women. Men may experience less social loneliness because they are expected to take the lead in social interactions and don't tend to find it as intimidating as women tend to.

More than Just a Feeling

Social and emotional connections don't just make us feel better mentally; they actually affect us physically. Researchers have discovered what they call "mirror neurons" in our brains that track the emotional state of people we're with and then mimic that state in our own brains. This is why moods are contagious: If our spouses are feeling sad, angry, afraid, ecstatic, playful, or what have you, we "catch" their feelings and begin to feel that way ourselves. In reality, our brains are absorbing, analyzing and decoding our spouses' body language, tone of voice, and other nonverbal communication at lightning speed, and we call the end result rapport, or being "on the same wavelength."

One of the most intriguing studies on the connection between biology and emotion involved women who knew that they were awaiting electrical shocks. Functional MRI scans showed that, when the women were alone, the brain regions associated with anxiety and stress were activated. This activity continued when a stranger held the women's hands, but it dropped significantly when their husbands held their hands. And when the activity in that area of the brain calmed down, the women reported feeling calmer.

Meanwhile, the physical pain that poets have for centuries attached to lost love may be more than just literary license. Some researchers theorize that social rejection is connected to the brain's pain centers. This could be a product of human evolution; survival depended on the strength found in numbers, and rejection from the group in prehistoric times was almost certainly a death sentence.

Building Social Networks

One theory to explain why married couples are less lonely is that the institution itself is more socially integrating. Married couples may be more likely to get involved in things like church, volunteer organizations, or activities geared toward parents like athletic booster clubs, for example. In other instances, though, marriage can be insulating; some couples just don't feel the need to build networks of friends and acquaintances because they are able to satisfy each other's requirements for social and emotional intimacy.

There is a trade-off in either case. Social involvement means obligations that can sometimes interfere with other needs and wants, and close friendship means investing some of your emotional capital outside your marriage. On the other hand, relying solely on your spouse to satisfy your social and emotional needs can set you up for extremely difficult adjustments should anything happen to end your relationship, or even change the nature of it, like an illness or accident. As with most other aspects of your marriage, the key lies in finding the right balance of "me" time, "us" time, and "us and them" time.

The Value of Friends

Like our spouses, friends help keep us sane by keeping us in touch with reality. (See Chapter 3 for more on staying sane.) Spending time with them allows us to look at the world from a different viewpoint. We can invite their input on the happenings in our own lives and see if their interpretation or reaction is the same as ours; we find out what's going on in their lives; we share laughter and support each other through struggles. Friends also allow us to pursue interests that our spouses don't enjoy. You might not care for fishing, and your husband might not care for musicals. But each of you enjoys these things more if you have someone to share it with. So you and your friend go to the musical, and your husband and his friend go fishing. Nobody resents being "dragged along," no one feels guilty about doing the dragging, and a good time is had by all.

Socializing together with other couples has its benefits, too. Like individual friendships, couple friendships give you a different point of reference for your own relationship and an opportunity to strengthen your bond. Stimulating conversation with another couple can reveal things you didn't know about your spouse; learning how another couple dealt with an issue you're facing now gives you a new perspective and may open up new options or ideas to you. Because no two people relate to each other in precisely the same way, you also learn more about relating to your spouse by observing other couples.

The Danger of Friends

Valuable and worthwhile as they are, friendships also have the potential to raise contentious issues in a marriage. When problems do arise, they usually come from one cause: comparison that devolves into competition.

Comparison is natural and can be a good thing. If you see that your friend's wife gives him a hard time about playing golf, for instance, you might be more appreciative of your own wife's "please do" attitude toward your hobbies. Likewise, seeing that another couple admires your husband's involvement in your children's activities can keep you from taking that involvement for granted.

When comparison is turned into competition, it often starts with praise for the other wife or husband and an explicit or implied criticism of your own spouse: the spick-and-span housekeeping of one wife compared to the more lived-in style of the other; the helpful-around-the-house husband compared to the one who watches sports all weekend; the couple who buys a new home with a pool compared with the one who is limping along with a ten-year-old car. Often, these competitive comparisons start with, "Why can't you be more like so-and-so?" and end in raised voices and slammed doors.

The secret to facing these challenges is to extract what you can use in what you learn from other couples and discard the rest. Your relationship is unique because each of you is unique. There is no one-size-fits-all formula for the ideal marriage, and what works for another couple might not be a good fit for you and your spouse.

. . . .

I'm Not Changing a Thing

Most of us have a natural resistance to change of any kind, mainly because it seldom feels like it's our own choice. When we were children, we were forced to submit to others' choices in so many ways, from what we wore, to what we ate, to when and where we played. As we grew up and began to make more of our own choices, we developed stubbornness to help us assert our own authority over making choices. As adults, our resistance is so ingrained that it becomes an automatic response to any outside suggestion for change. You can overcome your own stubbornness through self-talk: Tell yourself to forget making yourself change, and just let yourself change. This gives you the freedom to do what's best for you rather than trying to become a copy of someone else.

Crossing the Line

Friendships that violate boundaries can cause problems in your marriage, too. Boundaries protect your relationships with your spouse and your friends by defining appropriate behavior and respecting the differences between the marriage bond and the friendship bond. When you, your spouse, or a friend crosses the line, it can damage trust, self-esteem, and emotional intimacy.

Single Friends

Friendships between married and single people of the same sex can create friction in a marriage because the priorities of singletons and spouses are—or at least should be—quite different. Husbands might feel threatened by their wives' single girlfriends, especially those who are divorced, because they're afraid the friends are planting ideas of divorce in their wives' heads. Wives may dislike their husbands' single male buddies if the buddies encourage husbands to act as if they were single by staying out all night playing poker or going to strip clubs, for instance.

It helps to discuss your worries with your spouse. After all, your spouse knows his or her friends better than you do, and maybe what you imagine isn't at all close to how they really act when you aren't around. Such fears are common and normal, and bringing them into the open gives you both a chance to offer reassurance about your commitment to each other.

Maintaining a close relationship with your single friends might be challenging because of the differences in priorities. Your friends might not understand and may not be able to imagine what it feels like to bind your life with another; from the outside, they may feel you're making unwarranted sacrifices of your freedom and independence, and they just might not get that it doesn't feel like a sacrifice to you. Sometimes it can feel like you're trying to explain Mozart to someone who doesn't know what music is.

If you and your friends can accept each other's perspective without necessarily having to understand it, and without criticizing it, you'll probably be able to maintain the relationship without interruption. If, on the other hand, your single friends resent the fact that you're no longer the footloose party animal who could go out at a moment's notice, and you resent the fact that your friends don't seem to understand that you're married now, the relationship very likely will collapse on its own for lack of support.

Dealing with Jealousy

Our spouses' interactions with our own friends can ignite feelings of jealousy even in the best of us, because it's a very delicate dynamic and one that many of us harbor conflicting feelings about. We want our friends and our spouses to like each other, but we don't want them to like each other too much. If your husband and your girlfriend are laughing it up and having a grand old time, you might start to feel like the odd person out; if your wife and your best friend engage in a lot of thrust-and-parry banter, you might worry that it's really coded flirting.

This kind of jealousy is usually rooted in thinking of our spouses as possessions. Sometimes this is a conscious feeling, but more often it is subconscious, a throwback to our childhood days when older siblings could (and often did) take away from us anything at any time. The powerlessness we experienced then stays with us, and when we see our spouses getting along well with someone else, enjoying their company and having fun, we fear that they will be taken away from us, too.

The cure for this kind of jealousy is to remind yourself that your spouse has a mind of his or her own. No one can take your spouse away because your spouse makes his or her own choices, and he or she chose you.

Keeping Private Things Private

Even in this age of too much information, there are some things that should remain private between you and your spouse, no matter how close your outside friendships are. Details about things like your finances, your sex life, and personal demons should be guarded as carefully as you would protect any other precious thing. Divulging them to friends, even in jest, is a serious breach of trust. It can destroy the friendship and gravely damage your marriage.

The intimacy between you and your spouse is a rare and hard-won prize. Changing your role from confidante to broadcaster gouges a scar across that prize that may never fully heal. So, if you're tempted to share something private from your marriage with a friend, stop to ask yourself these things:

1. Did my spouse specifically ask me not to tell anyone this?
2. How will my spouse feel about this person knowing this?
3. How would I feel if my spouse told others things like this?
4. If I tell this person, will he or she tell others?
5. Will knowing this change this person's opinion of my spouse?

What if your friend presses you to cross this line? Some people do violate emotional boundaries—not with any hurtful intent, but just because they seem to be oblivious to them. It can be tricky to deflect these intrusions because most of us were raised to be truthful and obliging—two traits that conflict with protecting confidentiality, especially when we're questioned directly. Even if our first instinct is to reply, "That's none of your business," few of us actually come out and say it; it's too abrupt for most of us.

Fortunately, there are other ways to respond. You can use humor, saying with a smile, "That's kind of personal, isn't it?" You can turn the question around by saying, "Why do you want to know?" Or you can simply say, "I don't want to talk about that." If the friend still persists, you may have to tell him or her bluntly that the topic is off-limits. It's your responsibility to set and protect the boundaries between your marriage and your friends.

Friends add depth and breadth to our lives, stimulating us and inspiring us to expand our horizons. That extra texture in turn can enhance your relationship with your spouse, bringing half-hidden dimensions into sharp focus and giving you countless opportunities to appreciate anew the person you have linked your life with. In the right balance, social and emotional closeness with spouses and friends can help you stay physically and mentally healthy.

1. Talk with your spouse about how each of you feels about being alone.
2. Respect each other's needs for social time and alone time.
3. Encourage each other to develop appropriate friendships outside your marriage.

4. Protect each other's privacy.
5. Establish and enforce the proper boundaries between your marriage and your friendships.
6. Find ways to nurture and strengthen your emotional bond, which will in turn enhance your physical and mental health.

CHAPTER 5

Raising Healthy, Loving Children

Your healthy marriage is good for your children. According to research by Princeton University's Center for Research on Child Wellbeing, just the fact of being married can confer a host of benefits: Your children are less likely to live in poverty, less likely to experience violence, less likely to engage in risky behavior like having unprotected sex or experimenting with drugs or alcohol, and more likely to succeed in school. One study that followed a group of middle-class, highly intelligent white children through their seventies discovered that the divorce of parents sliced four years off the child's life expectancy. Other studies have shown that adult children of intact marriages have closer relationships with both parents and report fewer problems with depression.

Also, you and your spouse are less likely than unmarried parents to experience major mental health problems like depression and anxiety.

This is not to say that you won't spend a considerable amount of time and energy worrying about your children, or that the demands of parenting won't, at least occasionally, take a heavy toll on your relationship with your spouse. The challenge is not to create the perfect family, but to build a home environment that fosters support and solidarity, and in which every member of the family feels loved—even when they're driving you nuts.

. . . .

Lose Weight to Conceive

If you and your spouse are having difficulty conceiving a child, at least part of the problem might rest with your scale. A six-year Danish study showed that overweight couples are more likely to take a year or more to get pregnant. Overweight men tend to have lower levels of reproductive hormones and lower-quality semen, while overweight women may have problems with ovulation and early fetal development. The number of extra pounds makes a difference, too: Obese couples were three times more likely to take a year or more to conceive than normal-weight couples and twice as likely as merely overweight couples to try that long.

Great Expectations

Couples may talk about whether they want to have children, and they might even talk about when they'd like to start their family, taking into consideration such things as career demands and ambitions, debt and overall financial stability, and perhaps even who will be the primary caregiver. Yet most of us are woefully unprepared for the drastic upheaval that accompanies the irruption of a child into our lives. Men may resent the time and attention claimed by a newborn; women may feel unfairly burdened with the demands of being both a wife and mother. Fathers and mothers may have different notions of how to discipline children at various stages. They may even have different priorities for their children: One may feel that academic performance must be the top priority, while the other may feel that activities like sports, music, or theater should get equal consideration. Religious education may be quite important to one and not so important to the other. Even a seemingly minor thing like establishing a set bedtime for a grade-schooler can be a point of contention for parents.

. . . .

Juggling Work and Family

In the workplace, women are still perceived to have more family responsibilities than men. In a recent survey by Elle magazine and MSNBC.com, 15 percent of respondents said child-care responsibilities interfered with their female bosses' work, while only half that many said such duties hampered their male bosses' ability to do their jobs. You and your spouse might have to experiment to find the best way for each of you to maintain the fine balance between work and family responsibilities so that neither of you feels overly stressed or unfairly burdened.

It's impossible to predict every area of potential disagreement and resolve it beforehand. Life just isn't that orderly. But when you understand how being a parent affects your marriage, you can devise strategies to keep problems to a minimum for everyone.

Setting Boundaries

The instant you become a parent, you find yourself locked in the basic physics formula that says for every action there is an equal and opposite reaction. Your job is to set boundaries for your child to ensure his safety and well-being; his job is to challenge those boundaries at every opportunity. It's an eternal battle of wills, an unending power play, and the boundaries themselves are fluid according to circumstance.

Setting boundaries means more than placing limits on your child's behavior, though. It also means figuring out how to preserve and enhance your relationship with your spouse and how you will be parents together.

New Ways of Relating

When the impending birth of a child is introduced into a marriage, the couple has a whole new range of facets to explore about each other. Anticipation opens the door for sharing hopes and fears and for learning more about each other's tastes, wishes, insecurities, and expectations. Preparing the nursery, shopping for baby things, discussing feeding schedules and work schedules and family schedules, planning the finances and the baby's future—all these areas are rich fields for discovering some of each other's depths that may not have been revealed, or even relevant, before.

They also can reveal challenges for you. If Dad is expecting to hang around in the wings until the baby is old enough to play catch, and you're expecting him to take the 2 A.M. feeding every other night, there's likely to be some stress between you until you figure out a way to resolve your differences. Likewise, if you're spending most of your time planning for the baby with your mother or your girlfriends instead of with your husband, he is likely to feel frustrated or even used because his ideas and concerns don't seem to carry the proper weight.

. . . .

Babies Don't Save Marriages

In struggling relationships, the addition of a child tends to increase resentment instead of communication. A dependent spouse feels the baby displaces him in his partner's affections. A possessive parent tries to corner the baby's affection, excluding his or her spouse from crucial interaction with the child. An insecure parent feels overwhelmed by all the responsibility and may get defensive or withdrawn. An angry spouse finds more reasons to unleash her anger. An alcoholic parent seeks refuge in his or her addiction more often. Marital problems that existed before the arrival of a child are usually exacerbated afterwards, and they may require professional counseling to resolve.

Pay Attention to Me!

During the child's first few months of life, it's not uncommon for parents to neglect each other. When that pattern continues, the parents often find that, after the children have grown and left home, they have nothing left in common to sustain their marriage, and they end up divorcing after years, even decades.

It's a difficult line for parents to walk, because infants require so much time and attention—and, honestly, each of us only has so much time and attention to give. When each of you is happy to see your child's needs being met, the sacrifice of time and attention is hardly felt. But if either of you feels left out, pushed aside, or neglected, it's going to hurt your relationship.

Ideally, a well-balanced family is like an inverted triangle. Mom and Dad sit at the top corners, with the child forming the central point at the bottom. Both Mom and Dad are connected to the child, but they're still connected to each other, too. When the family is out of balance, the most common problem is a strained or broken connection between Mom and Dad.

The simplest, but not always easiest, solution to this challenge is to talk about it. You might have a hard time admitting that you feel like you're competing with your child for your spouse's attention and affection. Your spouse might dismiss your feelings as silly and illogical. If your spouse is demanding attention, you might feel unappreciated and overwhelmed, or you might take it as a criticism and get defensive or angry. Here are some things to remember if any of this becomes an issue in your marriage:

1. Recognize that your children place demands on each of you: physically, emotionally, financially, and temporally.
2. Accept that it's normal to feel overwhelmed occasionally.
3. Know that persistent feelings of being overwhelmed—or neglected, or what have you—are a sign that something is out of balance in your life.
4. Be honest with your spouse about your feelings, and be respectful of your spouse's feelings.
5. Trust your spouse to be honest with you and respectful of your feelings in return.

Sometimes the balance can be restored by leaving the children with their grandparents for a weekend or getting a sitter for a Tuesday night so the two of you can go to a movie. Sometimes that won't be an option, and you'll have to figure out another way to reconnect with each other. The beauty of it is that there are few rules; experiment until you come up with the method that works best for you.

Complementary Parenting

Balance is also important in the actual work of parenting, and it requires both of you. There's nothing like a child to bring out the fiercest parts of our personalities, and that can raise stress levels for everybody unless there is a complementary trait to soften the effects. The organizer, for instance, will try even harder to be organized amid the inherent chaos of child-rearing; the dreamer will brag about how smart and pretty the baby is; the perfectionist will do everything by the book and expect everyone else to follow protocol, too; the creative parent will find myriad ways to entertain the child; and the parent who doesn't feel quite grownup himself will feel overwhelmed and might end up working far harder than necessary to compensate.

The complementary traits that have served you well in the rest of your relationship can serve you well in parenthood, too. If you're an organizer, your spouse's spontaneity can balance your tendency to schedule everything. If you're a dreamer, your spouse's practicality can keep you well-grounded. If you're a perfectionist, your spouse's attention to emotional factors can mitigate potential problems. If you're the creative type, your spouse's consistency can provide the stability of some structure. If you're the one who feels like a kid taking on adult responsibilities, your spouse's support can give you the reassurance you need to feel more grown-up and capable.

The trick to balancing is to avoid criticizing each other. Criticism doesn't help; it aggravates. Instead, recognize each other's strengths and use them to complement your parenting the same way you use them to strengthen your relationship with each other. When each of you can work from your strengths, you both contribute to your child's well-being without putting undue strain on yourselves or your marriage.

A Different Perspective

We all experience a form of tunnel vision now and then—times when we just can't see any point of view but our own. When you have trouble seeing and appreciating your spouse's strengths, it's time to get a different perspective. Talking to a friend, a relative, a clergy person, or even a professional counselor can shift your viewpoint and help you see things in a refreshing light.

Using Parental Power

The question of how and when to use parental power has caused lively discussions (not to say arguments) among couples since the dawn of time. Sometimes parents don't know how to communicate their power to their children, and that frustrates everybody. Sometimes parents don't agree on which level of power is appropriate for a given situation; again, everyone ends up frustrated. And, often, parents don't share their power effectively, which results in the child usurping a great deal of power.

Communicating Power

There is only one phrase that effectively communicates your power to a child, and that phrase is, "I want you to . . ." But it feels harsh to a lot of us, and we don't want to be harsh with our children. We want to be kind, accepting, loving, gentle, responsive, and friendly, and those qualities just aren't conveyed by the straightforward, no-nonsense, "I want you to . . ." But consider this: Boundaries are about being safe, and children who learn to respect boundaries will have a much easier time adjusting to the multitude of limits they will encounter as adults. They'll have bosses who expect them to respect the boundaries of time by showing up when they're supposed to and getting their work done when it's due. They'll have coworkers who won't want them hovering around their desks, interrupting them. They'll have boyfriends or girlfriends who will need their own space and time to explore their own interests outside the relationship. And there are the social boundaries that prohibit dangerous behavior, and the prisons that loom for those who are unable or unwilling to respect those boundaries.

So, in the long run, and in your child's best interests, it is kinder, more loving, and more thoughtful to teach him or her to respect boundaries, starting with the ones you establish.

. . . .

Substitutes for Power

To avoid sounding harsh, parents will sometimes use different phrases to cajole their children into respecting boundaries. The problem is that these phrases often alert a child to opportunities to challenge your authority. For instance, if you say, "Stay in the yard," the child hears this as an attempt to control his behavior, and he may leave the yard simply to assert his own control. Threats like, "Stay in the yard or you're coming inside," and, "Stay in the yard or you'll get punished" also encourage the child to test you. Pleading ("Please stay in the yard") and bargaining ("If you stay in the yard, we'll go out for ice cream later") transfer power to the child. Only the phrase "I want you to" enables the child to understand that the power belongs to the parent and is not up for negotiation.

Degrees of Control

Perhaps the best illustration of how parents can differ in their approaches to setting boundaries and exercising power is the typical two-year-old—full of energy, eager to explore, getting into everything, and not terribly responsive to the word, "No." A single two-year-old can drive several rational adults crazy in an alarmingly short time.

Some parents want to contain the exploring child, putting him in a playpen or using baby gates or other gadgets to control the child's access to certain areas. Others might be more inclined to let the toddler roam, wanting to encourage the child's instinct to research, or wanting the child to experience the consequences of his behavior (within reason, of course), or enjoy the feeling of exploration and discovery, or experience his parent as a partner in his play. Differences in parenting styles can cause problems, or they can present opportunities for you and your spouse to learn more about each other and appreciate more deeply each other's strengths.

Sharing Parental Power

Parents have to set limits on children's behavior. Those limits can be spatial (stay in the yard, sleep in your own bed, etc.), temporal (be home by midnight, do your homework before dinner, etc.), or behavioral (don't jump on the couch, don't pull the dog's tail, etc.). To set these limits effectively, you and your spouse have to agree on them. Otherwise, if one of you is responsible for enforcing the boundaries and the other tends not to, your children will quickly learn to play you off each other. In addition, lack of agreement may lead to more polarizing differences in your parenting: The strict one may become ever stricter, and the lenient one ever more lenient. Finding a middle ground that establishes effective and reasonable boundaries protects both of you against your child's attempts at manipulation and reduces the potential for stress and frustration between you and your spouse. Let's look at some of the most common areas parents disagree on, again using that rambunctious two-year-old as an example.

How much leeway?

You might want to give your child as much freedom as possible in exploring his or her world; you don't want to set limits that the child would find frustrating and incomprehensible. Your spouse, on the other hand, doesn't want to have to watch the child every second to make sure he stays out of harm's way. Maybe he wants the child to develop a longer attention span by concentrating on one toy or task, or maybe he wants the child to learn early that there are boundaries.

Your different ideas here can offer lots of fodder for discussion:

- What do each of you enjoy most about watching your child explore?
- What gives each of you the most anxiety while watching your child explore?
- How do you feel about your own childhood experiences with exploring?

Teaching self-discipline

You might emphasize punishment as a way to teach your child that there are consequences for misbehavior—for instance, placing the child in a playpen as a punishment for playing with the TV remote. Your spouse might prefer putting things like the remote out of the child's reach instead of punishing him for playing with it, or he may even argue that, since there's no real harm in playing with the remote, the child shouldn't be deprived of it.

To better understand and resolve your differences, you might talk about:

- What you want your child to learn from your efforts to discipline him.
- What you fear if your child doesn't learn self-discipline.
- How your own parents approached the question of discipline and punishment.

No more tears

Maybe you just can't stand to see your child unhappy. You might use distraction rather than limits or punishment to steer your child away from unwanted behavior—getting her interested in a stuffed bunny, for instance, so that she forgets about the TV remote. Your spouse, on the other hand, might think it's better if the child learns she can't always do what she wants and that it's OK if she gets frustrated in the course of learning that. In this case, here are some things you and your spouse can talk about:

- How do you feel when your child is unhappy?
- How did your parents react when you were unhappy as a child?
- What do you think your child will learn from distraction techniques?

Dealing with difficulty

You might prefer to stand aside and let your child attempt to do things on his own, even if he isn't quite able to do it yet. Dealing with difficulty teaches perseverance and maybe even encourages creativity, you might feel. Your spouse, on the other hand, might prefer to make things easier for the child, so he can gain confidence from success, or so he won't get frustrated, or so he learns to accept help from others. Before your spouse accuses you of being mean and you respond in anger, try talking about these things:

- Is a task more fulfilling if it requires you to work hard?
- How do you feel when others offer to help you with something?
- How do you feel when no one offers to help?

Discussion is productive when you and your spouse make an effort to understand each other's position rather than viewing each other as unreasonable. Exploring each other's childhood experiences, the values you developed in consequence, the expectations each of you has for the other and for your child, the things each of you have learned about child-rearing, and your own feelings about being a parent—all of these provide endless grist for the discussion mill. An added bonus: Your marriage can be nourished by the presence of the new lives you two have created.

Loving Your Children

Most of us take for granted that parents love their children and that children know their parents love them. But the truth is that, all too often, children don't feel loved or understood because they don't recognize the way we express our love for them. Part of the problem is that we often forget that our children are not just miniature versions of ourselves; even in infancy, they are unique individuals, with their own ideas, feelings, expectations, and views of the world. It takes time and effort to get to know them.

Adding to this complex dynamic is the fact that siblings often seem like they're raised in different families. And they are, in the sense that each family is continually evolving as each family member continually grows and learns. Each of your children's personalities may develop in drastically different ways, and each may require a different parenting style from you and your spouse. Here's a quick look at some common personalities:

- **The little organizer.** This child functions best when she knows what the plan is for the day. She often is oblivious to the needs and feelings of other people. She hates intrusion, and she resents being corrected. Let her know that it's OK for her to be upset, but that being upset won't change anything. If she's shy about trying new things, tell her it's OK to take the chance of making a mistake.

- **The little helper.** This child seems to always be looking for approval, and his greatest reward is a sincere "Good job!" from Mom, Dad, or any other adult. He may develop a tendency to boast. He hates to disappoint and feels guilty if anyone is upset with him. He may become a follower and he may have trouble expressing his own thoughts and desires. Tell him it's OK to care about himself and that it's OK to take the chance of offending others sometimes. Don't fret that this will turn him into an obnoxious monster; with this type of behavior, knowing it's sometimes OK to offend leads to more assertive conduct, not aggression.

- **The little perfectionist.** Like the little organizer, the little perfectionist doesn't want to make a mistake and so can resist trying new things like learning to play the piano or trying out for the soccer team. But while the organizer wants to do things right so he won't be corrected, the perfectionist is afraid that others will get angry if she makes a mistake. Letting her know that it's OK to make someone angry might seem like bad parenting advice, but actually it gives this child the freedom to choose whether she's willing to risk making others angry. Also let her know that sometimes good is good enough, even if it isn't perfect.

- **The timid little one.** The timid child is afraid of being afraid, and your challenge as a parent is to let this child know that it's OK to enjoy being afraid sometimes. People go on rollercoasters, watch horror movies, read thrillers, and skydive for the rush of fear; they find it exhilarating to be spooked.

Sometimes the child who is afraid will actually put on a brave front, trying to prove that he isn't afraid. He's the child who will jump off the roof using a blanket as a parachute, or who will attempt to do a wheelie all the way down the block, or who will swim too far out in the lake. You might have to convince this child that it's OK for him to listen to his fears, because sometimes fear knows what it's talking about.

- **The "too little" little one.** Typically the youngest child (although not always), the "too little" child is nearly always swinging the pendulum between trying to prove how grown up he is and getting others to "do" for him because he's too little to do it himself. When he's trying to be grown up, he tends to make every task as difficult as possible. When he's trying to be "too little," he gets others to feel sorry for him. He rarely feels included or wanted, so he has to learn that it's OK to participate even if he isn't specifically invited. He might need to be reminded that it's OK to play sometimes; when he makes things difficult, he might need to be told that it's OK to do things the easy way as long as they're done correctly.

When you understand the quirks of your child's personality, you remove much of the stress that's common in parenting, and you promote a loving, stable environment for your whole family.

Finding Time for Everyone

Today's parents tend to lament the lack of quality time they can devote to their children. If you're feeling guilty or stressed about your hectic schedule, a University of Maryland study should cheer you up: Mothers and fathers actually spend more time with their children now than parents did in the 1950s and 1960s, the so-called golden era of parenting. On average, the study found, married mothers spend 51 hours a week with their children, four hours more than a generation ago, and married fathers spend 33 hours a week with them, a full twelve hours more.

Part of the guilt-inducing problem may stem from how you spend time with your children. If most of your family time is spent multitasking—watching television while eating dinner, for instance, or helping with homework in between answering e-mail—you might feel bad that you don't get enough one-on-one contact with your child. If most of your one-on-one contact involves hurrying your child to school or sports or music lessons, you might feel guilty that you don't spend time just getting to know about your child's activities, likes and dislikes, and so on. And if you're in the house while your child is outside playing with siblings or friends, you might feel guilty about not being involved enough.

The truth is, children and parents need all those kinds of time together. The trick is finding the right balance among family time, one-on-one time, and I'm-here-if-you-need-me-but-I'm-not-in-your-face time. Turning the television off during dinner is a simple way to keep all members of the family in touch with each other. You can make time for special outings, even if it's just a trip to the grocery store or a bike ride around the neighborhood, that can involve the entire family or just you and your child. And you can let your child know that, while you're available if he needs help, it's OK for him to do some things without you.

Children raised in healthy marriages, like their parents, fare better physically, mentally, emotionally, and financially. Studies show that children who feel loved are more curious, independent, and adventuresome than children who are insecure about their place in their parents' affections. They are less likely to be overly needy as adults and more likely to choose friends and romantic partners with whom they can develop healthy relationships. They also are more likely to remain close to their parents as adults— one of the many benefits of your healthy marriage.

1. Tell each other what you admire about the other's parenting style.
2. Share your hopes and fears about your child's future with each other, and figure out ways to minimize the fears and maximize the hopes.
3. Stay in tune with the balance of your family so you can keep Mom and Dad on an even keel at the top of the triangle.
4. Help each other focus on the things each of you does well in parenting, and draw on each other's strengths to complement your own.

CHAPTER 6

It's a Date!

The honeymoon is over. You and your spouse have settled into your life together. You know each other's habits, tastes, and preferences, and you've figured out how to work around them. Occasionally, something might come up to disrupt your schedule—an unexpected business meeting, or a sudden bout of illness, or even severe weather—but these times are pretty rare, and it doesn't take you long to slip back into the same old routine. Sure, it might be a little—boring, dare we say?—but it's comfortable, like a favorite pair of jeans or shoes is comfortable.

The thing is, your marriage isn't a favorite pair of jeans or shoes. Think of it instead like a classic car. You wouldn't neglect to change the oil and filters, check the belts, and switch out the spark plugs once in a while on a 1957 Chevy. Yet couple after couple neglects to perform the simple but regular maintenance every relationship requires in order to keep firing on all cylinders.

Here in the "Ever After"

Part of the problem is that nothing in our training prepares us for living day after day with the love of our life. Our fairy tales, fantasies, movies, and romance novels all concentrate on the courtship. If it's a happy tale, it culminates with the wedding and the lovebirds heading off into matrimonial bliss. Unhappy tales like that of Romeo and Juliet never make it to the bride's big day. Very little of our cultural reference (with the exception of soap operas, which bear even less resemblance to most of our lives than "Cinderella" does) explores what happens after you've been married for six and a half months, six and a half years, or sixteen and a half years.

As a result, we tend to be pitifully ill-prepared for the move from the courtship to the daily marriage, and it can be some time before we even notice the shift. We just wake up one day and realize that we can't remember the last time the two of us had a romantic dinner together, or even the last time we stopped to give each other a passionate kiss when we passed in the hallway on the way to our respective chores. We're comfortable with each other, more comfortable than we've ever been, and maybe we shouldn't expect any more than that. After all, we already know each other well. What else is there to discover?

The answer is "lots of things," if you make the opportunities to do so. Dating after the wedding serves the same purpose as dating during your courtship did: It gives you a chance to observe your partner in a different setting, under different circumstances, and gain vital insight into his or her personality. It's important to continue dating throughout your life together because, no matter how much time you spend with another person, there's always more to learn. But you have to make the effort.

The Down Side of Home

There's another important reason to keep dating with your spouse, and that is to get away once in a while from the host of unpleasant memories associated with home. Regardless of our romantic notions of what home is or can be or should be, it's the locus of several negatives for many of us. Home is where we have chores to do. It's where the idiosyncrasies of those who live with us annoy us the most. It's where we argue, where we discipline the children, where we struggle with finances, where we complain about work, where we don't have to be on our best behavior and often aren't. Just like when we were children, home is where we go when it's time to stop playing.

With all that weighing on us, it's virtually impossible to see our spouses as fun, playful, and interesting at home. We may appreciate everything our partner does around the house, but if we don't get to see them in front of a different backdrop now and then, we tend to start regarding them as part of the furnishings of our home life. Getting out of the house together, even if it's just a stroll around the neighborhood or a trip to the market, reminds us of each other's humanity.

Home as a Refuge

Home doesn't have to be a workhouse. Ideally, in fact, it should be a refuge for you and your spouse, a place where you can relax without being judged, where you can share your dreams without being ridiculed, and where you can unburden yourself of tension and aggravation without being punished. But because we have so many demands to meet at home as well as out in the rest of the world, it takes effort to build home into a place we look forward to going.

Why Aromatherapy Is So Popular

Smell is the most evocative of our senses. A whiff of fresh-baked bread can whisk us back to our grandmother's kitchen, even if we haven't been there for decades. If your home has a stuffy, stale smell or reeks of pets or gym shoes, it's hard to regard it as a refuge. Soothing and comforting smells at home help create a soothing and comforting atmosphere, so try using scented candles, potpourri, incense, or air sprays. To be most effective, and to avoid reactions like sneezing, scents should be subtle, not overpowering.

The good news is that it doesn't take a huge effort. It's really a matter of creating an atmosphere, and you can do that simply by what you say and how you say it. Positive comments create a positive atmosphere; negative ones, not surprisingly, create a negative atmosphere. Here are some examples of both:

- **Mmm, that smells good.** Compare your own reaction to this, as opposed to having someone wrinkle her nose and say, "Are you cooking something?" The latter almost automatically induces a defensive response, while the former makes you feel good.
- **I can't get comfortable.** Hearing this might make you feel guilty, like you should be able to help your spouse get comfortable, or that you're somehow responsible for your spouse's discomfort. Whatever your internal reaction, your spouse's physical discomfort thus vocalized causes you mental and emotional discomfort.
- **I like that color.** Even if you're referring to the color of the paint or the tablecloth, such expressions of liking radiate to encompass your partner. "I like" appeals to our desire for our spouses to be pleased, and if you're pleased about the color of the tablecloth, the subliminal message is that you're pleased with your spouse, too. Yes, even if he or she is not responsible for picking out the tablecloth.
- **I hate this song.** Just as "I like" statements convey liking your partner, whatever the actual subject, "I hate" statements convey dislike, which your partner is likely to take personally, even if only subconsciously.
- **You like this? Really?** Disbelief can imply disapproval, reminiscent of school days when anything out of the ordinary was rebuffed as "weird," "geeky," or otherwise unacceptable. As an adult, you can take the sting out of disbelief

by following it with a live-and-let-live statement; if you can spice it up with a little humor, so much the better.

If your partner is prone to making negative comments, try asking him or her to tell you what he or she likes. The phrases "Is there anything you like about this?" and "What do you like?" cue your partner to step back from seeing only the bad things and think about the positive.

Intricacies of Intimacy

Conventional wisdom divides intimacy into two broad sections, physical and emotional. Conventional wisdom further argues that women are more interested in emotional intimacy and men are more interested in physical intimacy. If it were that simple, the cure for couples who have trouble feeling close would be easy: Women would be urged to develop a stronger interest in sex, and men would be urged to develop a stronger interest in sharing how they feel.

In real life, however, intimacy is a much more complex creature, and creating and maintaining it is a constantly mutating challenge. Most couples connect on several levels. There is a physical attraction, but there also is an attraction of intelligence, because couples who don't find each other intellectually stimulating generally won't understand each other's humor, view of how the world works, priorities, or philosophy of life. There may be a spiritual attraction, and there usually is a recreational attraction, in that couples find common interests or hobbies and pursue them together. Married couples also are usually financially intimate, sharing not only their money but their financial goals and risks.

. . . .

Men Are Healthier with Intimate Relationships

Several studies have shown that people who have close, caring relationships have healthier hearts and cardiovascular systems, as well as less depression. Men may reap the most benefits. Yale researchers found that men who described their wives as loving and supportive experienced fewer artery blockages than men who did not feel loved and supported by their wives. Another study of 10,000 married couples showed a significantly lower incidence of chest pain over five years among men who said their wives "show their love."

How Do You Relate?

It is an axiom among counselors, therapists, and advice columnists that, if you don't like the way you're being treated, change how you act. We tend to get back what we give out, even if we aren't aware of it. Subconsciously, we cause people to treat us the way they do by the way we act and react.

The mechanism for this begins in childhood and our relationship with the parent of the same sex. This relationship teaches us to expect certain things from others. A boy whose father is critical, pushy, unfeeling, distant, or angry learns to subconsciously look for these same behaviors in other people. When this boy grows up, he's likely to seek out and marry someone who will deliver these behaviors for him, fulfilling his expectations.

Not only is his chosen bride capable of treating him this way, he trains her to do it. When she is kind, thoughtful, patient, loving, attentive, and helpful, he ignores it. She gets no emotional reward for these things, so she stops acting that way. On the other hand, as soon as she acts negatively toward him—criticizes him for a mistake, or gets angry with him—he pounces upon it with a forceful reaction. And even though it's not pleasant, the reaction itself is a reward; he's no longer ignoring her. He fails to nourish the positive behavior and reinforces the negative behavior, and in so doing, he trains her to act the way his father did.

Each of us is capable of a wide range of behaviors, and different people tend to bring out different behaviors in us. Some people bring out the worst in us, regardless of how much we resist giving rein to our lower nature. But in the company of some people, we behave so well we surprise ourselves. This is what many couples mean when they say, "I like who I am when I'm with you." In those pairings, the one partner brings out the best in the other.

Changing the Pattern

It is possible to break the cycle of causing others to treat us poorly. It requires changing the memories that trigger the cycle. One example is the case of a woman whose mother always steered the conversation toward herself. When the daughter wanted to talk to her mother about surgery she was about to have on her neck and the pain her neck was causing her, her mother started talking immediately about her own stomach pains and her fears that it might be cancer. After the conversation, the daughter felt as though her mother didn't care about her. With this pattern so solidly established, it's no surprise that this woman also was feeling that her husband didn't care about her.

In counseling, the daughter agreed to change her mother in her head. She told her subconscious to forget the memory of the actual conversation and instead imagined a new conversation in which her mother listened to what she had to say, showed concern, empathized with her pain, and finally gave her a hug and said, "I love you and I want you to be well." She used this as a substitute memory, establishing a new pattern for how she expected to be treated.

You and your spouse can use similar imagination techniques to change your own patterns. If your relationship with your own same-sex parent was difficult, choose an incident from your memory that you'd like to change, and then imagine it happening the way you would have liked. Whenever you think of your parent from now on, think of what you have imagined. You may be surprised to find that your spouse's treatment of you improves because your own behavior has changed to bring out the best in your partner.

It is easier, of course, to build and maintain intimacy on all fronts when you and your spouse are happy with the way you treat each other. Every aspect of intimacy requires trust, communication, acceptance, and caring, which can only thrive when each of you likes who you are with the other.

Dating Enhances Your Bond

Trust, communication, acceptance, and caring are fostered by bonding. Bonding is getting to understand each other's nonverbal communication. You come to understand this communication as you see it expressed in a variety of situations. Couples who have bonded well are able to read each other's nonverbal communication without having to hear it in words. Bonding is most easily maintained by sharing experiences, and it is easiest to share new experiences by getting out of the house together.

Dating by Yourselves

"Date night" doesn't have to be the same deal it was when you were in your courtship phase. Dinner and a movie might still be a good evening out for you, but there are plenty of other ways to date, and you don't have to limit yourselves to the usual agenda. In fact, the less rigid your definition of a "date," the more valuable your dating will be.

As we mentioned earlier, a date can be as simple as a stroll on a sunny afternoon, or as upscale as a four-course dinner and tickets to the opera. Wandering through a flea market or going to an air show, having a picnic or spending an afternoon fishing on the lake, bowling, ice skating, checking books out from the library—any activity you do together outside the home can qualify as a date.

Dating with Others

Group activities count as dating, too. Things like joining a softball or volleyball team, playing bridge, or even just going out to eat with another couple give you great opportunities to observe each other in a new light. Adding other people into the mix changes the dynamics of relating. The conversation will be different, responses will be different, and you're more likely to learn something new about your partner, or even just be reminded of a quality you had half-forgotten. Just as important, your spouse has the same opportunity to learn something new about you.

Dating with the Kids

Family dates are valuable, too. Your children benefit from seeing you and your spouse outside the home, when you're away from the pressures of housekeeping and homework. At home, the kids might not get a lot of opportunities to see your fun side; your love of roller coasters, for instance, isn't something that's likely to come up in the course of an argument over bedtimes. You get to see a new side of your children's personalities, too. Family bonding is just as important as couple bonding, so build a date schedule that includes whole-family activities as well as adults-only time.

Dating at Home

We've put a lot of emphasis on getting out of the house to date, but it is possible to date at home, too, especially if you're entertaining others. The introduction of outsiders into your home turns on the best you and your spouse have to offer, which makes the experience fun and interesting.

With a little work, you and your spouse can arrange dates for yourselves or for the whole family at home. You can have a game night, for example, or you can have an indoor picnic instead of sitting at the table for a meal. It requires more effort because it means changing your routine at home. Many of us simply don't have the time or energy to do that very often, which is why we recommend dating away from home. But if health issues or severe weather or other problems make getting out inconvenient or unworkable, you can call upon your ingenuity to create a date atmosphere in your own home.

Obstacles to Dating

What if you're all gung ho to date and your spouse kills the idea? It's not uncommon. Just think of virtually every sitcom you've ever watched: The wife wants to go dancing, and the husband wants to sit on the couch with his pants unbuttoned, watching a pay-per-view boxing match. Or the husband has invited friends over for dinner and expects the wife to be the charming hostess, even though she's got a nasty head cold. Television shows play these circumstances for laughs because they have an element of truth to them. Lots of us just seem to be on different wavelengths when it comes to dating our spouses. So let's look at some common obstacles to getting into the dating game with your spouse.

I Hadn't Planned on It

Some people just don't like doing anything unless they've had it penciled in on their calendars for at least a week. For these people, dating works best if it's a regular part of their schedule rather than a last-minute thing. Depending on how crazy your lives are with work and other commitments, you might find it works better to pick a regular "date night" and give it the same sanctity you give any other appointment on your calendar. If you can't manage to squeeze it in every week, make it the second and fourth Thursdays of the month, for example. If something comes up that will preempt date night, try hard to reschedule it as soon as possible; letting it slide can easily become a bad habit, and before you know it, you and your spouse will be slipping out of couple mode and back into roommate mode.

What Do You Want to Do?

Nothing puts the kibosh on a date like not being able to figure out what to do. If neither of you has any ideas nor can think of an activity that you both have the energy for, it's awfully tempting to skip date night altogether and spend another evening in front of the TV. One way to overcome the "what do you want to do" obstacle is to make a date grab bag. Make a list of all the activities you can think of; the only requirement is that they be away from home. Write each activity on a slip of paper, fold the slips, and put them in a jar, a paper bag, or some other suitable container. When you can't decide what you should do for date night, grab a slip from the date jar and do that activity.

I Don't Feel Like It

It's tempting to put date night off until we're in the mood to go out, but that can end up being a cop-out. If you really can't face going out in public because you're too tired or too cranky, schedule a make-up date night then and there. This reinforces your commitment to date, which is key to making it work for your relationship.

We Can't Afford It

If money is an issue, come up with things you can do together that are free or don't cost very much. Walks around the neighborhood and picnics are good activities when the weather cooperates. Some towns offer free concerts during the summer; some museums and art galleries have free or low-cost exhibits; matinee movies are cheaper than evening shows. Remember, too, that shopping counts as a date, so if you need to pick up some groceries or are thinking of getting a new sofa, you can make those your date activities without burdening your budget.

That Doesn't Really Interest Me

It's easier to agree on an activity when it's something you both enjoy, but there's enjoyment to be had by knowing your spouse is enjoying himself or herself, too. Joining your spouse in his or her pursuit of a hobby gives you a chance to find out why your spouse enjoys doing it and the aspects of his or her personality that the hobby brings out. You don't have to be a fan of kite-flying yourself to get some pleasure out of your husband's interest in the latest parafoil kite, and you don't have to be into gardening to enjoy watching your wife walk through the home and garden show at the fairgrounds, getting ideas for her own landscape projects.

In order to work properly—that is, to maintain and strengthen the bond you forged during courtship—dating throughout your marriage must be enjoyable for both of you. It should be something to look forward to and to savor. If it becomes an obligation, something to be endured like a pointless meeting at the office, it won't enhance bonding and, in fact, it may contribute to problems in your relationship. Activities that one of you enjoys and the other one dreads are best explored individually; for together time, make sure there's a reward for each of you.

Remember, too, that variety is essential to effective dating. If every date night is the same—same activity, same place, same interaction—it becomes as much a part of your routine as your time together at home. You discover more about each other when you see each other in different surroundings, doing different things, and responding to different stimuli.

In healthy marriages, there is no end to the bonding process, which means that there is no end to dating. Grandparents need to date as much as newlyweds do. Each phase of life brings new adventures and challenges, new things to learn, and new opportunities to broaden and deepen your understanding of your spouse. The more you discover about each other, the more you can enjoy the unique person walking through life with you.

Honey Do List

1. Make a commitment to spend regular dating time with each other.
2. Date in all the ways you can—just the two of you, with other couples, and as a family.
3. Do things you both like often.
4. Occasionally, go along with what your spouse wants to do and enjoy his or her enjoyment.
5. Build variety into your dates.

CHAPTER 7

More Fun in the Bedroom

Here's a truth you won't find much in the media (outside advertisements for erectile dysfunction medications): Married people have more and better sex than single people.

Really.

Oh, we know what you're thinking. You're thinking every single person out there is living a James Bond movie and every married couple out there is living "Leave it to Beaver." It's a popular misconception, relentlessly perpetuated by the mass media; a University of North Texas study found that 85 percent of the sexual behavior portrayed in movies was between people who were not married to each other. To further establish the stereotype of the nearly sexless marriage, this same study found that when sexual behavior did occur onscreen between married couples, the behavior usually consisted merely of passionate kissing. Implicit or explicit sex between married couples is rare in movies and television, and when it is portrayed, it usually is between married couples who are in their 20s and who don't have children.

But Hollywood has it wrong. So, before we go any further, let's smash some longstanding myths about sex and marriage. According to the National Health and Social Life Survey:

- Forty-three percent of married men reported having sex at least twice a week.

- Only 1.26 percent of single men who were not living with someone reported having sex at least twice a week.
- Single men are 20 times more likely to be celibate than married men.
- Single women are 10 times more likely than married women to have gone without sex in the past year.
- As many as a quarter of all single men and 30 percent of single women lead sexless lives.
- Half of married men describe sex with their wives as "extremely satisfying," while only 39 percent of cohabiting men gave that rating to sex with their partner.
- Married women are almost twice as likely to describe their sex lives as "extremely satisfying" as divorcées and never-married women.

While we're at it, let's define our terms. There are lots of phrases, idioms and expressions for sexual intercourse, but for our purposes here, we only need to use and define three: sex, sleeping together, and making love. Sex is the physical act of intercourse. Sleeping together is sex with feeling, some level of emotional connection. Making love is a bonding ritual that weaves physical, emotional, and psychological desires and commitments into one grandly fulfilling experience. Most couples engage in all three at different times. A quickie before the kids wake up on a Tuesday morning, for example, would come under our definition of sex, simply because there isn't time to do much more than take care of each other's physical needs. A longer session at bedtime that includes more kissing and touching would fall under the heading of sleeping together, because you have more time to establish your emotional connection while taking care of your physical desires. And the special, relaxed sessions you enjoy on a trip or a weekend when the children are visiting their grandparents, when you don't have any distractions and can really focus on each other, that's making love.

Sex Is Good for You

There's a strong body of evidence that sexual activity is good for your physical health as well as your emotional and mental health. A study by Queens University in Belfast, published in the *British Medical Journal,* found that, among middle-aged men, the death rate for those who reported experiencing frequent orgasms was half the rate for the less sexually active men. A follow-up study showed that men who had sex at least three times a week reduced their risk of heart attack and stroke by 50 percent.

Other studies have shown that sexual activity can contribute to weight loss and better overall fitness. Your body burns about two hundred calories during a really passionate session, similar to running for fifteen minutes. Your heart rate more than doubles, from an average of seventy beats a minute to 150, the equivalent of an athlete giving it his or her all in competition. Intercourse gives a workout to muscles in the thighs, buttocks, pelvis, arms, neck, and torso. And sexual activity increases testosterone production, which helps strengthen bones and muscles.

Exercise for Love

Maintaining a healthy weight is the one area where married couples tend to fare worse than singles. Aside from the health risks, extra poundage also can put your sex life at risk. Overweight men tend to have lower levels of testosterone, the hormone that influences sex drive in both men and women. Working out regularly not only can help you shed unwanted weight, vigorous exercise can stimulate pulses of sex hormones in both men and women, putting you more in the mood more often.

Need more convincing? A study of nearly three hundred women found that those whose partners did not use condoms were less likely to suffer from depression than those whose partners did use condoms. Researchers think this could be related to prostaglandin, a hormone that is found only in semen; it may be that prostaglandin is absorbed through the female genitalia and thus has an effect on regulating hormones in the woman's body. The higher levels of estrogen produced in a sexually active woman's body also may lessen the effects of PMS.

Sexual activity may also help you fight off illness and disease. Researchers at Wilkes University in Pennsylvania reported that people who have sex regularly—once or twice a week—have almost a third more immunoglobulin A, an antibody known to strengthen the body's immune system. There may not be a cure for the common cold, but sex may be able to keep you from catching a cold in the first place.

Finally, frequent orgasms may help protect men from prostate cancer, according to some urologists. The theory is that, to produce semen, a man's body takes a variety of elements from the blood, including potassium, zinc, and citric acid, which are significantly concentrated—up to 600 times—in the prostate and related areas; if there are any carcinogens in the blood, these would be similarly concentrated in the prostate. If a man doesn't ejaculate, these high concentrations of damaging and even cancer-causing elements are "stuck" in the prostate. But they are expelled from the body during ejaculation, so they can't do any damage. In fact, a study published by the British Journal of Urology International indicates that young men who ejaculate five or more times a week can reduce their risk of developing prostate cancer in later years by as much as 33 percent.

The Biochemistry of Sex

Our libidos are dictated by at least four different hormones and brain chemicals. Testosterone, which is present in both men and women, affects the strength of your sex drive; lower levels typically translate to less interest in sex. Dopamine, a neurochemical associated with the pleasure centers of the brain—and with various addictions, including drugs and alcohol, gambling, shopping, and so on—also affects sexual desire; high levels of dopamine mean high interest in sex. Prolactin is another neurochemical that acts as sort of an antidote to dopamine; it is, in effect, the "off" switch for sexual desire. Finally, there is oxytocin, the so-called "cuddle hormone." Oxytocin levels increase when you hold hands with or hug your lover; higher levels of oxytocin are associated with health benefits like protection against heart disease.

Dopamine

With normal levels of dopamine, we feel motivated and satisfied; we have realistic expectations, a healthy interest in sex, and a general sense of well-being. Excessive or insufficient levels of dopamine can interfere with your mental health, and therefore with your relationship. Too much dopamine can induce anxiety, aggression, compulsiveness, fetishism, and addiction. Too little dopamine has its own unpleasant side effects: inability to feel pleasure, inability to love, depression, lethargy, even physical problems like erectile dysfunction and sleep problems.

Prolactin

Although prolactin is necessary to tell you when to stop thinking about sex and do other things, excess levels can cause problems for both men and women. In fact, when your partner says, "Not tonight; I have a headache," he or she may really be suffering from high prolactin, which can cause headaches. Men and women alike are likely to lose interest in sex and may suffer from depression or mood swings. Men may become impotent or infertile; women may experience symptoms of menopause, even if their bodies are still producing sufficient estrogen. Both may gain weight, which can deepen feelings of depression. Going without sex for prolonged periods can cause prolactin levels to rise, which in turn decreases your interest in sex. There may be other causes, too, so be sure to talk to your doctor if these symptoms persist or worsen.

Oxytocin

Oxytocin stimulates the release of endorphins, the brain's natural painkillers. Right before orgasm, the amount of oxytocin in your body explodes to five times its normal level, releasing waves of endorphins that ease the pain of headaches, muscle aches, even arthritis and other forms of chronic pain.

. . . .

"I Need a Hug!"

Intimate touching—in the sense of warm, supportive physical contact, like hugging or cuddling on the couch—increases levels of oxytocin, a body chemical that helps reduce stress, promote longevity, and alleviate heart disease. Some researchers think the beneficent effects of oxytocin may explain why married people tend to be healthier than singles. Not only is there someone to hug you when you've had a bad day, but even unconscious touching, like spooning in bed, can boost your oxytocin levels.

The more you touch, the more oxytocin your body releases, which in turn increases your desire to touch and be touched. As your desire for touching rises, so do your levels of testosterone and dopamine, increasing your sexual desire. At this point, it's difficult for you to think of anything other than sex; you may even feel obsessed until you're able to satisfy your desire. Once you've climaxed, dopamine and testosterone levels drop, while prolactin levels rise. High prolactin levels make you feel physically satisfied so you can think about things other than sex. In fact, you may not feel any interest in sex or even in touching your partner until your prolactin levels ebb a bit.

Give More, Get More

If love is the desire to do good for your spouse, part of expressing your love is the desire to fulfill your spouse's needs in the bedroom. Research shows that we get a longer-lasting high from doing something for someone else than from doing something for ourselves. So, occasionally, ask your spouse what you can do for him or her. Then do it, even if it's not your favorite thing. Becoming a more giving lover likely will make your spouse more giving in return.

Understanding the biochemistry of sex is an important part of understanding your sex life with your partner. If your neuro-chemical cycle is out of sync with your partner's—and chances are it will be at least occasionally—the effects of that mismatch can lead to hurt feelings, resentment, and a host of other negative emotions. Keep in mind that, if your partner isn't in the mood, it doesn't necessarily mean the relationship is in trouble. It may be just a temporary imbalance of hormones and brain chemicals.

Sex Without Orgasm

Given the sense of closeness that higher levels of oxy-tocin can encourage, and the physical and emotional distancing associated with high levels of prolactin, some people advocate practicing "orgasm-free sex"—which covers everything up to and including intercourse, as long as neither partner climaxes. The theory is that abstaining from orgasm takes couples off the neurochemical roller coaster and allows them to create a more consistently loving and intimate relationship. If you and your spouse have a hard time finding a happy medium in your sexual activity and frequency—if, for instance, you go through periods of intense arousal and activity followed by periods where you barely touch each other—the neurochemical ebb and flow might be at least partly to blame, and you may find some relief by indulging, at least temporarily, in orgasm-free sex.

The Psychology of Making Love

Sex can satisfy our physical desires—the ones dictated by our biochemistry—but it is most fulfilling emotionally and psychologically when two partners make love. This happens when we're free of distractions, when we put aside our worries and are able to concentrate on our partner alone—how we feel about our partner, how being with him or her makes us feel, and how we can express those feelings. It is the most intimate of intimate acts, when both partners are fully engaged and focused on each other. These moments are when we feel safe, wanted, connected, and able to be accepted for who we are.

Admittedly, it can be difficult to work time for these moments into our increasingly busy lives, but that increasing busyness is precisely why it's so important that we do make time for intimacy. On some level, we all know this. It's why we plan romantic dinners and weekend getaways. It's why we send flowers or pick up a sentimental card for no particular reason; it's why we share a thirty-second dance to a favorite song on the radio before heading outside to mow the lawn or downstairs to fold the laundry. These are all ways of blocking off the myriad demands on our time and attention and confirming, however fleetingly, our partner's rank as "number one" in our lives.

Although it may culminate in the bedroom, making love actually begins with loving communication long before either of you even thinks of getting frisky. There's the smile on first making eye contact that says, "I'm glad to see you." There's the verbal greeting, the hi-honey-I'm-home that says, "I like you." There's the how-was-your-day small talk that says, "I'm interested in you." There's the let-me-help-you-bring-in-the-groceries-or-shovel-the-walk cooperation that says, "We're in this together." There's the exchange of humor and laughter that says, "I enjoy your company." And there's the comfortable silence that says, "I feel good being myself with you."

Housework and Sex

Something to think about the next time you and your spouse argue about whose turn it is to take out the trash: Research indicates a fair division of household chores equals more frequent and more satisfying sex. Wives who think the household duties are split fairly are more likely to report having sex at least once a week, while wives who think the division is unfair are more likely to have an affair. In fact, couples who don't think household responsibilities are properly shared are more likely to consider separating or divorcing.

Jammed Signals

Day-to-day frustrations can interfere with any of these levels of communication. You might be thinking about your son's poor performance on his math test and fail to look up and smile at your wife when she walks in. The phone might ring the minute you walk in the door, so you omit to greet your spouse; or, if you've had a particularly tiring or stressful day, you might say "hello" in a tone that really means, "I'm in a lousy mood." Your husband might have had a bad day at work, and while he's brooding on that, he fails to notice that you're struggling with three bags of groceries. Both of you may feel so worried about finances or that funny noise the dishwasher makes or your impending physical or any of a multitude of other things that your sense of humor has deserted you. And the silence between you may feel less like a healing poultice and more like a heavy blanket of unspoken resentment, irritation, and misunderstanding.

Memories from your childhood can also wreak havoc in your communication with your spouse. If your parents told you to smile even when you didn't feel like smiling, you may have developed the habit of "artificial smiling" as an adult, or you may not smile much at all. If your parents insisted that you act as though you liked someone even when you were angry with that person, you may find ways as an adult to convey your dislike or unhappiness even while you're giving a conventional greeting. If your parents discouraged your curiosity as a child—particularly by telling you to stop asking "why" or answering such questions with something like, "Because I said so"—you may have difficulty showing genuine interest in others as an adult, with the result that small talk becomes a recital rather than an interaction.

Do-Overs

We all have snapped at our spouses unintentionally, taking our frustrations out on them instead of directing them at the true source. Next time this happens, tap into your childhood for a technique to stop the misdirection from escalating: Ask for a do-over. Instead of snapping back (or continuing the snapping, if you're the one who started it), step out of the room for a few seconds, then come back in and say to your spouse, "Can we start over?" Then say what you really wanted to say to your spouse in the first place: "I had a rotten day today, and I need to vent," for instance, or even a neutral, "Hello."

> A do-over gives you both space to regain your equilibrium and prevents outside frustrations from sparking a pointless marital spat.

Cooperation requires agreement on what is to be done, recognition that a task will be accomplished more easily with assistance, thoughtfulness, and respect for the other person's abilities. This can be tough if your childhood was rife with moments when you were forced to agree with your parents or caregivers whether you wanted to or not; as an adult, you may look for ways to disagree instead when these childhood memories are triggered. Similarly, you may reject your spouse's offer of help if you had to fight as a child to show older siblings or adults that you could do something yourself; alternatively, you might resist offering your own assistance, assuming your spouse feels the same way. On the other hand, if you always had to help younger siblings when you were a child, you may carry that behavior into adulthood, taking over tasks instead of assisting in them.

Humor, which is really the main form of playfulness for adults, can be stifled by childhood memories of being told to quit playing and get to work. And if you were often chided by your parents or other adults for being too boisterous in your play, you might have difficulty allowing your playful side to come out as an adult.

Feeling good just being yourself may be the toughest thing for most adults. We have to overcome a whole host of memories and insecurities, and we have to learn to trust our partners with who we are. The obstacles come from times, usually dating back to childhood, when someone—a parent, a teacher, our peers and even our good friends—let us know that being ourselves was not acceptable. Sometimes it's a continual message; more often, it comes when we make an ill-conceived joke, ask an obvious question, or are angry, thoughtless, or unkind. The moments themselves may be miniscule compared with our regular behavior, but the message that it's not OK to act that way or feel that way is immeasurably powerful and long-lasting. So we learn to put on an acceptable façade, and we are very careful not to let it slip.

No One Is a Mind-Reader

Honest discussion about your sexuality—what you like, what you don't like, what you'd like to try, and what you fantasize about—is just as critical to your relationship in the bedroom as honest discussion about any other topic is to your relationship overall. Neither of you can know what really turns the other one on if you don't talk about it. If it's hard for you to articulate what you want sexually, try starting the conversation with a question: "Is there something you'd like to try that we haven't done yet?" Once your spouse opens up, it will be easier for you to follow suit.

The thing is, that façade doesn't do us any good in the bedroom, where we are the most vulnerable. If we don't feel safe being ourselves with our partners, sex becomes a duty, an obligation; it's not something we look forward to, and it may even become something we try hard to avoid. It certainly never rises to the level of making love, because you can't truly make love if you're wearing a psychological mask.

Unjamming the Signals

Now, before you start thinking it's impossible to overcome all these obstacles to really making love with your spouse, there's good news: All you really have to do is think about it. Ask yourself these questions. Is it OK for me:

1. To enjoy my spouse?
2. To like my spouse?
3. To be curious about my spouse?
4. To agree with my spouse?
5. To play with my spouse?
6. To be myself with my spouse?

The answer to each question, of course, is yes. We all know that the answer should be yes. It is inconceivable that the answer could be anything else, right?

But if you have difficulty answering yes to any of these questions—if you struggle internally because you know yes is the right answer but you just can't bring yourself to say it, or your instinctive answer is something like, "Yes, but . . ."—then you know there is something getting in the way of your ability to enjoy, like, be curious about, agree with, play with, or be yourself with your spouse. And once you're aware that something is getting in the way, you can figure out what it is and how to get around it.

Men Fake It, Too

Women have always been suspected of faking orgasms à la Meg Ryan in *When Harry Met Sally*. But men fake it, too. According to a poll by British ITV's *This Morning*, almost 20 percent of men admit faking an orgasm; in 18- to 34-year-old men, the figure is 43 percent. On the other hand, more than half—56 percent—of married people said they have genuine orgasms with their spouses.

Men fake it for the same reasons women do: They don't want their partners to feel bad. It's one of those "little white lies" that many of us feel is OK, but in marriage, it indicates a breakdown in communication, or at least a failure to build communication. Achieving orgasm isn't always necessary to enjoy sex, but being able to feel good about yourself even if your partner doesn't orgasm requires honest communication and a high level of trust.

Leaving the Past in the Past

Unpleasant memories associated with sex can interfere with enjoying an adult sexual relationship. These unpleasant memories might come from religious training or your parents' attitude toward sex, or they might have more traumatic roots—in past abuse, for example. Many of these things, and especially the effects of sexual abuse, may require professional counseling to be dealt with effectively.

Sometimes people make valiant attempts to overcome their distasteful associations with sex. One woman who had been abused as a child used mental pornography to tame her aversion to having sex with her husband. This tactic worked for a while, in that she was able to participate in sex, but she wasn't able to enjoy it until she sought counseling to deal with the effects of the childhood abuse.

There are other strategies: the proverbial headache, the on-purpose fight right before bedtime. Sometimes people use alcohol or drugs; it's the only way they know of to "get in the mood."

Guilt can interfere with your enjoyment of sex. If your religion prohibits premarital sex and you violated that stricture, you may have trouble enjoying sex with your spouse, even though it's acceptable under your religious beliefs. If you have trouble forgiving yourself for your earlier transgression, it might be helpful to consult a member of the clergy.

. . . .

"Everybody Does It!"

A recent study by the Guttmacher Institute indicates that, contrary to popular belief, premarital sex has been the rule more than the exception for some sixty years. Nearly nine in ten women born in the 1940s had premarital sex, and, based on the 38,000 people surveyed in the study, researchers said roughly 95 percent of Americans engage in premarital sex by age 44.

Parental attitudes can be contagious, too. If your mother frequently said, "Men are all the same—they only want one thing," you might find yourself feeling quite critical of your husband, especially when he's a little frisky. It might help to ask yourself, "Is it OK for my husband to be the way he is?" If the answer is yes, you can overlook the little things that inspire your criticism. If you have trouble answering yes, there may be some behaviors that are absolutely unacceptable to you; counseling may be warranted to help you figure out why and what to do about it.

The Science of Attraction

Researchers, fashion designers, and the editors of women's magazines have been trying to determine for years exactly what attracts men and women to each other and how we can boost our own attractiveness. Some people say it's pheromones; we put out a scent that attracts the opposite sex. Some people say that's baloney; they argue that human noses aren't sensitive enough to detect pheromones, especially under all the scented soaps and shampoos, deodorant, perfume, and aftershave we douse ourselves with. Some say it's just a case of opposites attracting, like a pair of magnets, but recent research indicates people tend to be attracted to those who are most like themselves. A couple of studies have even tried to determine whether body type influences attractiveness by manipulating things like a woman's waist-to-hip ratio or body mass index.

The science of attraction can be confusing, but there are some things that seem pretty clear. One is that women like men whom other women find attractive, and men don't like men who are attractive to women. A University of Aberdeen study illustrated this by having women smile at certain men and not at others. The man being smiled at was rated as more attractive by other women and as less attractive by other men. The researchers said this phenomenon is seen in other animals, too, where females look for mates that other females find desirable, while males dislike the competition represented by other, attractive males.

Meanwhile, men seem to be more attracted to symmetry than to any other single factor in a woman's appearance—good news for women who have spent years worrying about whether their favorite pair of jeans makes their butt look too big. Fashion designer Bradley Bayou, author of *The Science of Sexy*, says women should stop obsessing over what they think they lack and flaunt what they do have. Choose clothing that makes you look balanced and even, regardless of what the current fad is. If you've got large hips and a tiny waist, for example, select A-line skirts and tailored tops to show off your hourglass figure.

And, it turns out your mother was right when she told you that what's inside is more important than what's outside. Various studies have shown that women who were rated average or below average in appearance before certain personality traits were observable soared in perceived attractiveness after men got to know them better. What are those traits? Kindness, confidence, energy, cooperativeness, and a sense of humor—the very things that contribute to loving communication outside the bedroom and lay the foundation for one heck of a good time in it.

1. Keep communication lines open with each other; good communication lays the foundation for satisfying sex.
2. Give yourself permission to explore your sexuality with your spouse.
3. Give your spouse permission to explore his or her sexuality with you.
4. Make time for all kinds of fun in the bedroom: sex, sleeping together, and making love.
5. Let yourself feel good by making your spouse feel good.

CHAPTER 8

Reining in Cheating Hearts

If women's magazines are any indication, cheating is one of the top worries couples have.

But research indicates married people take their vow of "forsaking all others" seriously. Men who live with their girlfriends are four times more likely to cheat than husbands are, and women who live with their boyfriends are eight times more likely to cheat than wives are. In addition, a Pew Research Center survey showed that nearly nine in ten Americans consider it morally wrong for married people to have an affair; only seven in one hundred say it isn't a moral issue.

That isn't to say that we're all models of fidelity, of course, but if self-reporting is to be believed (and it's admittedly difficult to know how honest people are in answering these sorts of questions), adultery is far from the norm. Some estimate that as many as one in four married people cheat on their spouses. The National Science Foundation funds the General Social Survey, which puts the number lower: In 2004, the survey reported that only 15 percent of those who had ever been married admitted having sex outside their marriage. Men are slightly more likely to admit to extramarital affairs than women (20 percent of men versus 12 percent of women). The gender difference in admitted affairs seems to square with gender differences in attitudes toward affairs: The Pew survey found that men are somewhat less likely to consider cheating immoral than women are.

Still, many of us will, at some point in our marriages, at least worry that we or our spouses may be tempted to stray. Following the principle that forewarned is forearmed, we look now at what leads some of us into affairs, strategies for dealing with temptation, and tips for working together to get past an affair and build a stronger relationship.

Testosterone Related to Cheating

Researchers have found that men's testosterone levels fluctuate according to whether they are single, in a committed relationship, or in a committed relationship and cheating—or even considering cheating. Single men and those who would consider cheating on their partners had higher levels of testosterone, which may help them compete with other men for mates. Men in committed relationships who would not consider cheating had lower levels, which researchers think may help those men form closer attachments to their partners.

The Path to Infidelity

Ask ten marriage counselors what leads some people to cheat on their spouses, and you'll get at least five different answers. Some research indicates that women will cheat if they're unhappy in their marriages for a year or more, while men who admit having affairs report being quite happy in their marriages. Other research indicates that many affairs are accidental—the product of proximity to an attractive man or woman, the thrill of a new relationship, the inability to resist exercising our power of attraction. Still other research indicates that some people are hard-wired to cheat, and those studying the question point to mounds of evidence showing that sexual monogamy is extraordinarily rare in the animal kingdom, even among species previously thought to be monogamous.

There are actually three kinds of affairs, each with its own trigger. There is the affair born of commitment phobia, which often occurs within the first few years of marriage, and sometimes within the first months or even weeks. There is the proverbial midlife crisis affair, usually committed by the husband and brought on by a sudden shift in priorities. And there is the narcissistic affair, in which the straying partner has a string of flings and seems oblivious to the damage these affairs do to the marriage.

"You Made Your Bed . . ."

Commitment phobia is the fear of being trapped and often is rooted in childhood experiences of not being allowed to change one's mind, of being told, "You made your bed, now you must lie in it." Marriage feels like a trap, so the person who suffers from commitment phobia keeps one foot outside the marriage by having sex with other people. This kind of affair usually doesn't involve an emotional attachment—that would be another trap—but instead consists of one-night stands. Interestingly, if the marriage becomes unpleasant, the affairs often cease because the person who strays no longer feels trapped; he or she now has an excuse to leave the marriage.

This is what happened with a couple we'll call Leo and Phoebe. Leo experienced his commitment phobia almost immediately after the two married; he felt angry toward her on their wedding night, although he didn't know why. A few weeks after they were married, he went out bowling with his buddies, met a woman, and had sex with her. When he got home, he told Phoebe that he and the boys had gone out for a beer and had ended up talking long into the night.

Phoebe bought Leo's story until one of her friends told her what had really happened. She was furious. When she confronted him, Leo acknowledged the indiscretion and blamed it on his being drunk. So Phoebe focused on his "drinking problem" to keep him from doing it again. He had a couple more one-night stands, and she became more angry, more controlling, and more accusatory.

Leo stopped having one-night stands, and Phoebe thought he stopped because she was controlling him, so she continued her antagonistic behavior. They became adversaries, with Phoebe playing the accuser and Leo denying any wrongdoing. You might think this would drive Leo away, but in fact it was just what he needed to overcome feeling trapped. He stopped cheating because his marriage was miserable, so he no longer felt trapped; he had a good excuse to walk away from the relationship, so he felt free to stay.

He even found ways to make her angry at him. He used obnoxious humor, left his dirty clothes on the floor, hid money from her, and refused to do simple repairs in order to fuel her anger. Her anger kept him free from his commitment phobia. If she brought up his affairs, he'd tell her she should forget about them because they were in the past—and this statement angered her even more, because it dismissed the hurt he had caused her.

Commitment phobia may be at the root of much domestic abuse. The wife (or husband) may be so committed to having a happy marriage that she is nice to him no matter what he does. In trying to get her to be angry at him, he becomes abusive, verbally and then physically. When the violence escalates to the point of her calling in the authorities, he becomes repentant and promises he will not do it again. And he is sincere because, at this moment, his commitment phobia is gone. It returns when she puts it all behind her to have a good relationship with him; he has to make her angry again, so the cycle starts over.

Sometimes these relationships last for years, occasionally even lifetimes. Outsiders wonder why they stay together when they are so angry and so unhappy with each other. They don't realize that this couple needs the anger and unhappiness to even be together in the first place.

That's not to say couples in this kind of situation must put up with the misery brought on by commitment phobia, but it typically is not something that will resolve itself. The betrayed spouse has the power to change the dynamic by insisting his or her partner get professional help for the underlying fear that creates all the other unhappiness.

The Midlife Affair

As trite as it is, the midlife crisis affair is more than just a stereotype. Marriage counselors report that it is the most common type of affair they see in their practices. It occurs after fifteen or twenty years of what appears to be a good marriage, and it can be devastating because it involves not only sexual infidelity but an emotional straying. One spouse develops an affectionate relationship with someone else, often a coworker or friend of long standing, and its onset is sudden, often escalating within days. Emotion rises rapidly to an extreme high. The person feels love as he (or she) never has before, certainly not with his spouse.

The emotional high begins to decline almost immediately, and as it does, the person in the throes of the crisis seeks ways to regain the high. This is usually when the cheating spouse and his or her new love interest engage in sex for the first time. But nothing recaptures the initial high because it was artificial to begin with, the effect of past experience and changing priorities. This kind of crisis lasts about three years, and, depending on the patience of the betrayed spouse, the marriage may survive and even be stronger and healthier afterward.

The triggers for the midlife affair usually lie in the hurt of a past relationship. A young man who is deeply in love is rejected by a young woman, and he is devastated. As he copes with his broken heart, he decides he will never let anyone hurt him like that again. In effect, albeit subconsciously, this decision means he will not let himself get that close to anyone again.

He moves on and eventually meets another woman whom he asks to marry him. He doesn't fall in love with her, but he is afraid of losing her the way he lost the other woman, so he convinces himself that he will learn to love this woman. The marriage usually is nice but a bit superficial, because it doesn't involve his emotions too deeply.

Fast-forward fifteen years or so, and the emotions he has buried for so long are ready to erupt. One day, his coworker says something or brushes against him or looks at him in a way that opens the floodgates to those feelings. He feels like a teenager, giddy and thrilled and confused and excited in ways he has never before experienced. The affair has started.

It should be noted here that marriages born of this type of affair rarely last; as many as 75 percent end in divorce within just a few years. This is because the emotional high of the first days of the affair leads to unrealistic expectations. When the high wears off and cannot be recaptured, there is nothing else to sustain the relationship. The first marriage, even though superficial, worked well because the straying spouse didn't have overblown expectations.

Sometimes this kind of affair is stopped before it starts because the spouse who is about to be cheated on gets angry with the spouse about to cheat. This kind of preventive fury may be more common than anyone knows, because couples who avert an affair this way are unlikely to seek counseling. If the affair isn't prevented, and if the betrayed spouse waits for the affair to run its course, the marriage often can be saved, although counseling may be needed to work out the issues arising from the original rejection and the damage caused by the affair.

Are Men More Likely to Cheat in Midlife?

Women are not immune from pursuing midlife affairs, but men may be more susceptible because of a change in priorities that often comes around age forty. For the first twenty years of his adult life, a man typically is focused on building his career and creating financial stability for his family. Once he is established, he is ready to make the relationships in his life his top priority. But the people he wants to be close to aren't there any more. The children are grown and doing their own thing. His wife, having spent years taking care of the family, wants to focus on her own interests. The man is eager to do all the bonding he hasn't had time for until now, and no one is around for him to bond with. In these circumstances, the friend or coworker comes as a welcome release for those pent-up feelings.

The story of Elvin and Maria shows how the midlife affair can come about. They had been married for twenty years. They had a nice relationship—not exciting, but pleasant. They never argued; they took care of the things that needed taking care of; they were good parents to their children.

One day Elvin said he was going to help Joan with a leak in her kitchen sink. Joan was a divorcée, not very attractive but with a pleasant personality. Maria saw nothing wrong with Elvin helping her; in fact, she was proud of his thoughtfulness, especially as Joan didn't have much money. It wasn't long before Joan had other repair jobs for Elvin. There was the hinge on the screen door, the broken chair and the furnace that would not stay on. Still, Maria thought it was OK. Even when Elvin told her about Joan confiding in him about her bad marriage and the trials of her life now, Maria was glad Elvin was willing to lend a sympathetic ear.

That something wasn't quite right began to dawn on Maria when she noticed that Elvin would abruptly hang up the phone when she walked into the room. Sometimes, when she was out, she would call home, expecting him to be there, and he wasn't. He became distracted, staring into space while ostensibly watching television and asking her to repeat things because he hadn't been listening.

Finally, it became apparent that he was having an affair with Joan. Maria was shattered. She concluded that she had been inadequate as a wife, that she had not paid enough attention to her husband—in short, that it was her fault he had turned to another woman. She turned to therapy for herself. She gained insight, became more loving, probed her psyche for subconscious drives that made her neglect her husband.

The affair continued. Elvin talked about leaving the marriage but made no overt moves to do so. Interestingly, he felt comfortable talking with his wife about his affair because she was so understanding. Then, after several months of this, the affair seemed to fade away. The surreptitious phone calls stopped. The repairs at Joan's house became less frequent. Elvin began putting off his visits, and when he did go, he no longer spent hours there. He started taking more interest at home. The affair had run its course.

Maria asked Elvin to enter counseling, and he agreed. In therapy, he was able to deal with issues from more than twenty years earlier, when he had been painfully rejected by a woman he dearly loved. Maria's patience—that is, her willingness to wait the affair out—and Elvin's work in counseling allowed them to salvage their marriage and build a closer, more loving relationship than they had had before.

Narcissistic Affairs

The prognosis for getting a narcissistic cheater to change his or her ways isn't good. This is because the narcissist blames others for whatever he or she does. It isn't her fault she cheated; it's her husband's fault for neglecting her, or it's her paramour's fault for pursuing her. Spouses take the brunt of the blame, though, for not being loving enough, not being good enough in bed, not paying enough attention to the narcissist's needs—pick a reason. Narcissists feel no shame, guilt, or even responsibility for what they have done, and they have no idea why their spouses should be so upset. In their thinking, spouses should just forgive them and go on from there. Unfortunately, when one spouse refuses to take responsibility for his or her actions and the effects of those actions, there seems to be little hope for salvaging these marriages.

Yet, spouses of narcissists often hang in there for years and years. The narcissist is very good at giving plausible explanations for the transgression (without, of course, accepting any personal responsibility), making promises, and otherwise being kind to the injured spouse. This behavior often convinces the spouse to stay and hope things will get better. They don't, but it can be very difficult for the betrayed spouse to realize this, especially if he or she accepts the blame, even subconsciously, for the other's behavior. Professional counseling may be required to help the betrayed spouse see the situation in its true light.

What If You Really Are the Pursued?

Sometimes a friend or coworker crosses the line and makes a pass at you. How do you respond? Most of us, recalling our parents' strictures to "play nice," try to find a way to shrug off the pass, saying something like, "What if your wife heard you say that?" If that doesn't work (and it often doesn't), we might say, "It's not right," or even, "Please don't do that." We're trying to reestablish our boundaries while obeying our training to be nice. And, somewhere deep down, we may feel flattered and pleased at the attention, even if we have no intention of violating our marriage vows. The problem is that by being nice, we may inadvertently send mixed signals to the transgressor, hinting that our protests don't really mean that the behavior is unwelcome. If you want to protect your marriage and preserve the proper relationship with the friend or coworker, you have to set your boundaries clearly, concisely, and forcefully. When the friend or coworker says or does something inappropriate, say, "Stop it," as sternly as you would correct a child's misbehavior. Remember, you don't have to be nice in this situation.

A woman we'll call Ann was in this kind of situation. She met Jerry in high school. They fell in love and got married shortly after graduation. Just a few weeks before they were to be married, Jerry had sex with another girl. Ann found out about it and was troubled, but she forgave him so they could get married.

This was the beginning of a troubled marriage that would go on for more than thirty years. Ann had demonstrated her willingness to accept Jerry's behavior by staying in the relationship after that first episode. He had numerous affairs over the years, and even left Ann a couple of times to live with another woman. He always came back, and he always expected to be taken back. After all, Ann had forgiven him the first time.

Jerry was the youngest child in a large family. By the time he came on the scene, his parents, especially his mom, were tired of disciplining children. Everything Jerry did was OK, and if it wasn't OK, his parents put the best possible spin on what he did. He was always a "good boy," regardless of what he did. He did not learn to have personal boundaries, feel guilt over anything he did, or care about how someone else felt.

Ann grew up in a dysfunctional family with an alcoholic father. She watched her mother enable her father's drinking, holding supper for hours until he came home (drunk), covering for him, enduring his unpleasant behavior with patience, never betraying anger. By example, Ann learned to endure what her husband did so their marriage could endure.

Ann did confront Jerry about his affairs, but it did no good. Jerry had learned well that whatever he did was OK, that he should not be held accountable, and that his wife should be accepting of him. When Ann complained about his behavior, his response was that she needed to forgive him. There was no expression of regret or repentance.

Ann carried a heavy burden during the years of their marriage. She did what she could to keep the marriage together, and though she was understandably depressed during those years, she could find no way to resolve the issues. Eventually, through therapy, she was able to understand the situation and develop a healthy caring for herself, which convinced her to end the marriage. She decided it was better to be alone than in this relationship.

Unfortunately, this is often the way relationships with narcissists end. Narcissists will not take the initiative to change—after all, in their minds, they are doing nothing wrong—and they will resist most effectively any pressure from others to change. Because there are varying degrees of narcissism, it might be possible to save some relationships, but the outlook is difficult and success by no means assured.

Virtual Cheating

In this day and age, no discussion of extramarital affairs can be considered complete without touching upon cyber sex—hooking up with a stranger on the Internet and exchanging erotic e-mails or instant messages. Some people argue that, because the two people online never actually meet or touch, cyber sex doesn't count as cheating. But talk to the spouses of those who engage in cyber sex, and you'll find that the effects of "virtual cheating" are the same as if the two had arranged a lunch-time tryst at a seedy motel. Moreover, according to the Center for Internet Studies in Connecticut, about half the people who engage in cyber sex progress to telephone contact with their online partners, and up to a third will meet their online partner in person at some point.

The triggers that lead to online affairs are similar to those that lead to real-life ones, although sexual compulsion may play a more significant role in cyber cheating. Signs of cyber cheating include secretiveness, spending an inordinate amount of time on the computer, especially when the spouse is asleep or not at home, and lack of interest in family activities, home maintenance, and so on.

Coping with the Aftermath

An affair changes everything. No matter how we may try to rationalize it away—and the betrayed spouse is just as likely to rationalize as the betrayer—the wounds created by an affair are deep and slow to heal. There is a loss of innocence: The trusting spouse can no longer take it on faith that his or her spouse will live up to the marriage vows. There is anger that the person who made those promises to you did not care enough about your feelings to resist temptation. There is guilt—the guilt of the cheating spouse for causing the damage, and sometimes the guilt of the betrayed spouse for failing to prevent the affair. And there is grief for all that has been lost.

The first step is to acknowledge that this isn't a mere scrape to be healed with a Scooby Doo bandage and a kiss. The pain won't last forever, but the scars will change the landscape of your relationship. Accepting that you cannot go back to the way things were before allows you to move ahead when you're ready.

Marriage counselors say that more than half their clients are motivated to seek help by an affair. Professional therapy may be essential to repairing your relationship, because it can help you identify problems that have laid beneath the surface for each of you. Counseling also prompts you to step outside your immediate emotions and look at your relationship, your spouse's behavior, and your own from a different perspective. Sometimes therapy is most effective when you and your spouse attend sessions together; sometimes it's more effective for each of you to schedule separate sessions. If both of you are willing to find the formula that works for you and have the patience to let yourself, your spouse, and your marriage heal, you can eventually get past the transgression and concentrate on building a stronger, more loving relationship.

Preventive Maintenance for Your Marriage

A good marriage may not be good enough to stifle the urge to stray. According to several studies over the past twenty-five years, the difference between being merely "pretty happy" in your marriage and "very happy" translates into a twice-as-likely risk of infidelity, and people who are "not too happy" with their marriages are four times more likely to cheat. Even "very happy" spouses are more likely to have an affair than those who rate their marriages as "extremely happy."

It would seem, then, that—as in so many areas of life—prevention is more effective than treatment. Here are some techniques to make sure you and your spouse aren't just settling for an OK relationship:

- **Make dating a lifelong habit.** Dating gets you out of the house together and gives you time to see the fun, interesting side of each other's personalities. Your relationship can soon feel old and stale if you don't have an opportunity to see each at your best. (Chapter 6 is devoted to the concept of lifelong dating.)
- **Make sure you connect with your spouse every day.** Maybe your schedules are so crazy that you barely have time to kiss each other good-bye in the morning, but don't

neglect to give each other that kiss. Even a quick, tender touch on the arm as you're moving from one task to the next is better than no contact at all. Five-minute phone calls to catch each other up on the day can help keep you connected, too.

- **Set boundaries with others to protect your marriage.** Give yourself permission to be forceful with friends or coworkers who might encroach on your boundaries. Avoid situations or conversations that you would feel awkward telling your spouse about. Make your marriage your first priority, and insist that others respect it.

- **Set boundaries for your children, too.** Resist the urge to be an uber-parent at the expense of your relationship with your spouse. Teach your children when it is appropriate for them to claim your attention and when it isn't, and insist that they respect the boundaries you set for them. Remember that you and your spouse are the foundation of your family; you can't keep your family whole and healthy if you let the foundation rot away.

- **Set goals for your marriage together.** Share your dreams and your fears. Compare your strengths and weaknesses. Talk frequently about the things you'd like to accomplish, individually and as a couple. Envision your relationship five, ten, twenty years from now, and discuss ways to get where you both want to go. Life may be unpredictable, but plans and goals that each of you is invested in keep you grounded in the relationship and help reinforce the bond that keeps you pulling together.

As we noted at the beginning of this chapter, relationships require routine maintenance to stay at the top of their form. Neglect the maintenance today, and you run the risk of deeper, more costly problems showing up tomorrow. Tend to your marriage, though, and you can rely on it to pass virtually any test it might encounter.

1. Find small, regular ways to maintain your connection with each other.
2. Clearly mark the boundaries of your marriage to each other, to your children, and to outsiders.
3. Nurture your relationship by sharing your vision of what you want your future together to be.
4. If an affair threatens your relationship, seek professional counseling, either individually or as a couple.

CHAPTER 9

Fighting Right

In any relationship of any length, there will be conflict. You and your spouse might clash over money, children, in-laws, vacation plans, friendships, or a host of other issues. And a big part of the conflict might be the immutable fact that you and your spouse may have different approaches to thinking about these things. It is important to understand your partner's way of thinking rather than assuming he or she thinks the way you do—or *should* think the way you do. He may be a risk taker while you value security and predictability. She may worry about what other people think while you couldn't give a snap what anybody else thinks. He may want to get every detail right, and you may want to get things done so you can move on. She may want to induce self-discipline in the children when you want the children to be carefree. He may want to be frugal while you want to spend money to enhance your lifestyle.

All these differences can be sources of conflict when each of you demands that the other change. One couple currently in counseling has been married 35 years. They haven't dealt creatively with their differences over the years; rather, each of them has become entrenched in his or her own thinking. Now, they have reached the point where the marriage is breaking up. The differences became more and more pronounced over the years until they reached the point where it is very difficult to reconcile them.

It didn't have to be this way. If they had dealt with each other rather than trying to enforce their own wills or hide their conflicts, they could have grown in their relationship rather than getting to a point where there is little hope of salvaging their marriage. This is an object lesson about how dealing creatively with conflict can be a source of enrichment for both of you as you expand each other's thinking.

Getting Over the Fear of Anger

One of the reasons many couples try to gloss over areas of conflict is because most people are afraid of anger in others. Our first encounters with anger came when we were children, small, weak, and helpless, and angry people were extraordinarily frightening. Here was this giant adult towering over you, making this terrible, scary face, yelling so loud it made your little ears hurt, and your first instinct was to run away and hide until this angry ogre went away. Even after the adult calmed down, you felt timid and uncertain, afraid the anger and all the scary things that go with it would return. It took a while for you to recover your equilibrium.

As adults, most of us still have this visceral reaction to anger. When those around us seem irritable, we tend to watch our step, hold our tongue, and sometimes hold our breath until the other's mood improves. We've never gotten over our fear of anger.

But the strategies we used to feel safe in the face of anger (or potential anger) as a child don't work very well when we're grown up. Especially in marriage, if we walk around on eggshells, hold back on conversing, and give other signals of being uneasy or tense, our partners often pick up subliminal clues that we expect them to be angry, and then they are angry, although they may not be able to figure out why. In this kind of marriage, the rough edges aren't smoothed down; instead, they continue to cause abrasions, leaving each spouse wounded and scarred.

Our childhood fear of anger stemmed from a perceived (or, sadly, sometimes real) threat to our safety. An adult's anger seemed life-threatening to us, and that's the memory we carry with us into adulthood. But, except in abusive relationships, expressions of anger from and toward adults do not threaten our physical safety. (See Appendix A: Staying Safe for information on the cycle of physical abuse and its effects.) There is no need for us to run in fear from an angry adult now. Instead, as adults, we need to recognize the difference between real dangers and perceived dangers. Only when we know the real danger can we adopt effective strategies for dealing with it.

Too often, the first thing we think of when we consider a course of action is whether it will make our partner angry. But that is rarely the real danger. The real danger in spending money foolishly, for instance, is not that your spouse will be angry but that you won't have enough money to pay the necessary bills—the things that shelter, feed, clothe, and protect your family. Likewise, the real danger in having an affair is that you could destroy your marriage, and the real danger in quitting your job is that you won't have an income and might not be able to replace it. Certainly, your spouse may be angry in any of these or dozens of other situations, but that isn't the primary danger.

Self-talk can help you move from your childhood fear of anger to fear of real hazards. Remind yourself that you are an adult among adults, that you do have real dangers to face at every stage in life, and that anger is not the real problem.

· ·

You Can Handle It

Conflict is by definition adversarial, a contest with an expectation that there will be a winner and a loser. When you and your spouse are in this mode, you take turns attacking each other and defending yourselves, but you don't have a chance to move beyond that to resolving the issue at hand. Self-talk can help you step away from adversarial mode. By telling yourself, "Turn on the part of me that knows how to handle this," you may find that the negative energy of argument disappears and is replaced by the positive energy that lets you be in tune with your spouse and creative in finding solutions.

Over the course of your marriage, you and your spouse are going to make each other angry many times. But, because of the nature of marriage, you can learn to get past the anger to the true danger behind it, and once you've figured out how to do that, anger is no longer anything to be frightened of.

Coping with Conflict

When you're no longer afraid of anger, conflict isn't as scary, either. You can disagree without being afraid that your spouse will get angry. That said, there are several ways to "fight right" when conflicts do arise, ways that will enable you and your spouse to see each other's point of view and reach a workable solution rather than digging in your heels and refusing to budge.

Get Out of the House

This seems counterintuitive: We tend to feel private discussions should be confined to our private space—our home. But when sensitive issues arise, emotions often run high, interfering with our ability to come up with creative solutions. Getting away from home helps temper that emotionality because it cues us to turn on our "public" behavior. We tend to be more polite, more willing to listen, and more respectful of others in public than we are in private—all behaviors that enable constructive conversation and problem-solving. Find a restaurant with a secluded booth, an unfrequented corner of the park, or any place away from home where you can talk things through. If you've got a really complex issue to sort out, consider going to a motel for a weekend to give yourselves plenty of time to work through it.

Listen to the Nonverbal Cues

The lion's share of what we say isn't in our words; it's in our body language, facial expressions, and tone of voice. When you pay attention to your spouse's nonverbal cues, you can cut past irrelevancies and get to the heart of what's really going on in the current conflict. Saying things like, "You look tired," "You sound angry," and so on lets your partner know that you're paying attention to his feelings, and that can be enough to help your partner identify why he feels the way he does.

Hostility begets hostility. You can break the cycle by learning to interpret your spouse's emotional expressions and responding, not with your own emotional expression, but in a way that moves the discussion forward. Some examples:

- **"You always . . ." or "You never . . ." statements usually are an expression of frustration.** Instead of arguing about the frequency of the behavior at issue, acknowledge the emotion behind the statement by saying, "You sound frustrated."
- **Profanity is often used to shock.** Instead of arguing about the language, defuse the tension by saying something

like, "It sounds like you want to shock me." This simple acknowledgement often ends the profanity, because it's hard to shock someone who knows you're trying to do it.

- **Criticism is a terrific mechanism for expressing bad feelings and building hostility in a discussion.** Instead of arguing about whether the criticism is justified, you can get to the feelings behind the criticism by saying, "You sound like you're hurting." Your spouse then is able to derive some comfort from the indication that you care about how he or she feels.

- **Demands are another way of hiding true feelings, especially fear.** Arguing about whether the demands are reasonable keeps you locked in the hostility cycle. Instead, you can say, "It sounds like you're scared." Your spouse may in fact be hoping that you'll do something to rescue him or her emotionally, and acknowledging the fear can help both of you move toward a resolution.

- **"Loaded" words usually indicate anger, and again tend to escalate the hostility if you respond to them as if they were logical communication.** Instead, you can say, "You sound like you're angry," which allows your spouse to feel you understand his or her emotions.

Agree First

You may disagree with 99 percent of what your spouse is saying, but before you start ripping apart her argument, focus on the 1 percent of common ground. When you first mention where you agree, you encourage your partner to look for other areas where you can agree. Another plus: Agreeing first helps defuse the frustration that often accompanies disagreements because you have re-injected the hope of further agreement.

Thank Your Spouse

You may indeed be contributing to conflict by having done something wrong yourself. But apologizing doesn't always lead to true reconciliation; instead, offering an apology might make your spouse feel obligated to extend forgiveness, even if he or she is not quite ready to give it willingly. Instead of just saying you're sorry and expecting forgiveness, you can recognize a good quality with which your partner responds to you: "Thank you for your understanding (or patience, kindness, or especially love) when I did that." This approach lets your spouse feel affirmed in his or her legitimate complaint, even as he or she keeps on loving you—even though you did something you shouldn't have.

Don't Put Off until Tomorrow . . .

Giving in to your natural instinct to avoid confrontation actually can cause more damage in the long run than the conflict itself. When resentment, hurt feelings, and frustration are allowed to fester, you inevitably pull away from each other, losing not only the intimacy you've worked so hard to create but also the flexibility that allows you to overlook each other's foibles—and perhaps even find humor and enjoyment in them. Your bond with your spouse is like a rubber band: If it is stretched too far too often, it will eventually lose its elasticity and, with it, its ability to keep the two of you close. Under constant tension, even if that tension is unacknowledged, your bond may even break. What follows are some strategies to help you keep small grievances from getting out of control.

When You Should Put It Off

Sometimes it's better to delay a contentious discussion until you feel calmer. In the heat of the moment, it's easy to say things we don't mean because we don't take the time to choose the right words. Instead, you can say something like, "I need a break," "I'm too upset right now," or, "I don't have the energy to go into this now." It's important that you make a date to discuss the issue later; otherwise, your spouse is likely to think you intend to avoid the discussion altogether. Setting a specific time to talk about the issue allows both of you to step back and figure out ways to better communicate your thoughts and feelings. "I'm too upset now. Can we talk about this after dinner?" tells your spouse how you're feeling and what you need, while providing assurance that you aren't ignoring the issue.

The Humor Shield

Nothing squelches rising tension like a well-timed dose of humor. But it has to be wielded carefully so as not to wound. The most effective way to make sure your attempt at humor won't be misconstrued is to use it on yourself, or on the situation.

Let's say the grievance is your husband's habit of putting his dirty clothes on or near the hamper, but not *in* it. And let's say that, even though you've asked him dozens of times to correct this behavior, you still end up picking up his clothes from the floor every laundry day. You could exclaim, in a justly irritated tone, "Why can't you put your clothes in the hamper, for heaven's sake?" or accuse him of being a slob. Or you could make your point like this: "Thanks for giving me the opportunity to do my bending and stretching exercises again, honey." Or: "In a really well-designed house, there would be a hamper built into the floor." If you can laugh off a minor annoyance, chances are your spouse will, too, and humor provides the release you need to prevent that particular tension from building.

Choosing Battles

Not all annoyances are worth even the energy it takes to laugh about them. Exercise your ability to decide which things really get under your skin and which things fall under the heading, "It's not my first choice, but it's not that important to me." When you make a conscious decision to let go of your irritation, you actually instruct your subconscious mind to ignore the thing that triggers it. So, going back to our dirty clothes example, if you decide it isn't worth your energy to complain about it, you'll find that, after a while, it's just something you've come to accept.

The key here is a two-step process: First, you have to remember that you do have the power to decide what bothers you and what doesn't (something we all tend to forget from time to time). Second, you have to make the decision to let go of the things that you aren't willing to invest your energy in.

Drama Kings and Queens

Some of us just aren't very well-suited to a quiet life. We get bored if things stay on an even keel for too long, and we are overcome by an irresistible urge to rock the boat. If both you and your spouse enjoy a good row now and then, that's OK. Problems tend to arise, though, when one of you is a drama freak and other isn't; the nondrama freak doesn't understand the drama freak's need for or enjoyment of an argument and tends to feel emotionally exhausted by them rather than energized.

This was the problem for one couple, who otherwise were quite compatible and happy together. She didn't feel the need to fight over little things, but every so often, her husband would go out of his way to start an argument, usually by picking at her until she finally snapped back. For the first couple years, these arguments ended with her in tears and him in the garage, fuming about how hard it was to communicate with her. Then one day, the wife changed her strategy. She asked her husband point-blank, "Are you trying to start a fight?" His "yes" wasn't just flippancy; it was the truth. "OK," the wife said, "let's fight." The husband burst out laughing, and the wife started laughing, too. Later, they discussed why he enjoyed an occasional argument, and the wife made a conscious decision to try to enjoy arguing, too. Now that she recognized the symptoms of her husband's fight-withdrawal, she could approach those times with interest and humor instead of her usual defensive, angry posture. The result: This couple ended up having lots of "fun" fights that usually ended in laughter (and very often resolved minor grievances for each of them) and very few serious fights that threatened their relationship.

Confronting the Bully

Years ago, I met a couple whose relationship had begun as potentially abusive. They had been married for twenty years, and they were obviously a very close, loving, and devoted couple. When I asked their secret to their happy marriage, the wife responded that she was "hard to live with," and the husband agreed. It doesn't sound like the basis of a good marriage, but what it really meant was that she refused to tolerate abusive behavior from him right from the beginning. If she had backed down and tried to appease him, their life together would have been a very different story.

I have seen many women who were in potentially abusive marriages but who were not abused, and the difference in each case was the woman's reaction to the abuse. Typically, their husbands hit them or otherwise abused them once, and the women told their husbands the marriage would end if it ever happened again.

By sticking up for themselves, they were able to show the abusers that the thing they feared most—the loss of the relationship—was sure to happen if they continued their abusive behavior.

Note to Reader

Not all partners who hit you once will stop, no matter how much you stand up for yourself. If you are in an abusive relationship, or if you think you might be, please turn to Appendix A: Staying Safe. There you will find information on identifying abuse, the cycle of abuse, and places to go for help if you need it.

These women also shared another trait: They recognized that they were not responsible for their husbands' actions. Abusers often play on our sense of guilt, arguing that they wouldn't "have to" hit if only we would do this, that, or the other. If we accept this reasoning, we fall into the trap of believing we can control someone else's behavior by the way we ourselves behave. If we were nicer, more loving, more understanding, more (insert adjective here), he wouldn't get mad and beat us, goes our thinking. The abuse then feels like it is somehow our fault—which is exactly what the abuser wants us to believe, because we won't leave if we think we're at least partially responsible for the problem.

Getting Out of the Victim's Role

In any conflict, the common struggle is between winner and loser, victor and victim. When it looks like we might become victims, we tend to react by feeling bad. This is how we've been trained since birth: If we feel bad enough long enough, eventually somebody will come along and make us feel better. So when we have a conflict with our spouse, our tendency is to keep on feeling bad until our spouse makes us feel better. This is why so many marital arguments start over trivial things; the conflict is symbolic, not substantive.

The way out of this feel-bad-to-feel-good cycle is to forget making yourself feel OK and just let yourself feel OK. Once you've given yourself permission to feel OK, your need to win the argument and defeat your spouse is gone; there's nothing to sustain it any more.

The abuser uses anger to intimidate his victim. The victim automatically does what she thinks is necessary to placate her persecutor, thus inviting the abuser to continue his ways. After all, it's working. Why should he stop? It's when it stops working that he might actually change. In fact, he often does change, at least temporarily, when the police get involved, but if the victim continues trying to placate him, he'll soon be back to his tried-and-true methods of control and intimidation.

Effective confrontation is not an easy skill to learn. It requires overcoming your own fear of anger and being willing to be "hard to live with." It may, and often does, require professional counseling to deal with your fears and the effects of abuse, which, unfortunately, can linger for years. Counseling also can help you recognize whether there is hope for building a better relationship or whether you would be better off to leave it.

Conflict in your marriage doesn't necessarily mean you're in an abusive relationship, and it doesn't mean that conflicts are destined to escalate. However, it does take effort and understanding to turn conflicts into opportunities for growth in yourself and your relationship. When you address your conflicts immediately and creatively, you and your partner can learn new things about yourselves and each other, and this new knowledge in turn creates a nurturing environment where conflict is neither feared nor exaggerated. Thus is born a new, positive cycle of behavior that strengthens and deepens your healthy marriage.

Honey Do List

1. Do what you can to see each other's point of view.
2. Pay attention to each other's nonverbal cues and address them.
3. Find common ground first; then work on cultivating more.
4. Tackle issues as soon and as honestly as possible.
5. Be willing to be hard to live with; only you can stand up for yourself.

CHAPTER 10

Building a Healthier Life Together

Since the latter part of the nineteenth century, researchers have known that married people tend to live longer than singletons. But why that should be so is a mystery that has only recently begun to be resolved, and there is still a sort of chicken-and-egg-conundrum quality to the question. Are married people healthier, and therefore longer-lived, because healthy people are more likely to marry than unhealthy people? Or does marriage confer some unique benefit that makes people healthier?

Recent research indicates there are several components of the marriage relationship that promote better health and longer life. Married couples tend to encourage each other to eat better, exercise more, and kick harmful habits like smoking. The emotional bond and support between husband and wife helps reduce stress, which can adversely affect the immune system. Intellectual stimulation, at home and out in the community through activities like bridge groups, civic organizations, and church involvement, helps ward off physical ailments like dementia and mental health problems like depression.

We must note here that these findings apply only to happy marriages. In unhappy marriages, the research indicates, these health benefits are not only absent but may in fact be reversed. That is, spouses in an unhappy marriage experience more stress and more depression, are more likely to engage in unhealthy behaviors like smoking and overindulgence in alcohol or other drugs, are less likely to be involved in community activities, and thus are more likely to suffer from heart disease, depression, and lowered immune system responses.

There's no question that every marriage experiences some times of stress and some times of unhappiness. Happily married couples recognize those times as temporary phases and are able to weather them secure in the knowledge that the foundation of their relationship remains stable. If the foundation is unstable, however, the bad times can cause deep rifts that require a great deal of work, even professional counseling, to heal. Whatever the state of your marriage, there are steps you can take to promote the elements of your relationship that contribute to a longer, healthier, happier life together.

. . . .

Hold Hands, Cut Stress

The stronger the bond between you and your spouse, the better health you're likely to enjoy, according to recent research. Supportive touching—holding hands, hugging, even cuddling on the couch—increases levels of the calming hormone oxytocin in both men and women. People with higher levels of oxytocin have lower blood pressure and lower heart rates and report lower levels of stress and anxiety.

Love Is in the Ear of the Listener

The most important ingredient in a healthy relationship is love, and there are myriad ways to express our love. We might make a special dinner, or bring home flowers for no reason, or arrange for a sitter on a week night so we can have an evening alone together, or any of dozens of other acts of kindness. All these are ways of showing our partners how much we value them.

Unfortunately, what we intend as such an expression isn't always received that way. In fact, quite often our expressions of love make our spouses feel less rather than more valued. You know the result of such miscommunication: Your spouse feels frustrated and injured, and you feel unfairly condemned and even rejected (or vice versa). Suddenly, instead of being partners facing the world together, it feels like you're standing on opposite sides of a deep chasm, with no way of bridging the gap.

Don't panic. This is one of those areas where a little knowledge about the intent and the actual effect can do wonders to improve your communication. And that will help you close the chasm between you.

"I Worry about You"

Some of us believe that worrying shows how much someone means to us; after all, it takes a lot of mental and emotional energy to worry, and we wouldn't bother to expend that energy if the object of our worry wasn't dear to us. On some level, we may even feel guilty if we don't worry enough about our partner.

The problem is that worry often feels like a burden or even an insult to the adored (and worried-about) person. Saying, "I was worried about you," when your spouse is late getting home from work, for example, can feel like an attempt to make him or her feel guilty for not calling to let you know about the delay. It also can suggest a lack of confidence in your spouse's ability to take care of himself or herself, to deal with a particular situation, or to act appropriately in a given set of circumstances. Most of us expect our parents to worry about us, even when we're well into adulthood. But when our spouses worry about us, we tend to feel like we're being treated like children, and we resent that from people who are supposed to be our peers.

What to do about it

If you're the worrier, try changing the way you express your worry. Instead of saying, "I worry about you," identify what you're really worried about: "I'm worried about the weather," for example, or "I'm worried about the traffic in the city." This way, you express your concern for your spouse's well-being, which lets you feel good, but you don't denigrate your spouse as the actual cause of your worry.

If you're the worried-about, you can respond to your spouse's worry with a smile and a quick, "I love you, too." It shows that you understand the real message your spouse was trying to send; in fact, it forces you to interpret it the way your spouse intended it. An added bonus: It prevents an irritated response like, "I can take care of myself," which can become the opening salvo in a needless argument.

"I Agree with You"

For some of us, agreeing with our spouses feels like expressing love for them. But our spouses don't always see it that way. In fact, constant agreement without any discussion or evaluation can make the one being agreed with feel pressured because agreement means the final decision-making responsibility rests entirely on her shoulders. Or he may feel unimportant because the agreeing wife doesn't even take the time to assess what he says; she just smiles and nods. If there is no dialogue, just agreement, she can't feel engaged, and if there is no discussion, he can't get any direction or guidance from her.

Close Relationships Protect the Heart

A 2004 British study of patients who had suffered heart attacks found that those who had at least one close relationship—whether it was a spouse, sibling, or best friend—were 50 percent less likely to die of heart problems in the year following their first attack. The "loner" patients, on the other hand, were more likely to have more severe heart attacks and suffer more complications. The loners also were more likely to have had a history of heart ailments than the connected patients.

What to do about it

If you are the overly agreeable one in your marriage, chances are you're afraid that disagreement will signal some more serious discord, or that your partner won't like you. But it's possible to present a different point of view without being rude, dismissive, or otherwise unlikable. In fact, chances are your spouse will like you better if you express your own opinion rather than just going along with whatever is suggested to you. If you just can't bring yourself to disagree, try asking your spouse why he or she holds that particular opinion. At least you're engaged in the process, and even if you end up agreeing, your spouse likely will feel that your agreement is genuine rather than reflexive.

If you are the perennially agreed-with, asking your spouse to explain why he or she agrees with you can open the discussion door. Beware, though, of responses like, "I trust your judgment," because those kinds of statements will shut the door again. You can come back with a playful, "What if you didn't trust my judgment? Would you still agree with this decision?" Overcoming your spouse's tendency to agree automatically might require some real effort on your part, and it's important not to get irritated or angry if that happens. Remember that agreement, at least for your spouse, is intended as an expression of love, and disagreement doesn't come naturally to him or her.

"Why Don't You . . . ?"

The perfectionists among us express their love by showing us how to do better. They figure that, because they long to achieve perfection, everyone else does, too, and part of their responsibility to their nearest and dearest is helping them toward that goal. So they are willing, even eager, to point out our mistakes and flaws and offer suggestions on how we can improve. These suggestions might come in any area: our choice of clothing, our work habits, our diets, our favorite radio station—pick a topic, and chances are the perfectionist in your life can nitpick it.

Well, that's what it often feels like to the corrected, anyway. Continual criticism is unlikely to make anyone (other than a fellow perfectionist) feel loved. On the contrary, the recipient of these "helpful suggestions" is very likely to feel discouraged, resentful, and even indignant at what is perceived as unfair criticism or blame. Eventually, the nonperfectionist spouse may just give up trying to satisfy the perfectionist, feeling that there's no point in pursuing an impossible goal. The perfectionist, meanwhile, does not understand any of these reactions and feels misunderstood (and therefore unloved) in the face of them.

What to do about it

If you're the perfectionist, try giving yourself a new rule: You must say at least three nice things on a given subject before you offer any criticisms. A bonus to this strategy is that it forces you to think in complimentary terms, something perfectionists tend to be not very good at. Telling your husband he looks good in his new suit takes a lot of the sting out of saying he's overdue for a haircut, and complimenting your wife on her diligence in getting the oil changed every 3,000 miles makes her much more receptive to the suggestion that she should start having the tires rotated, too.

If you're living with a perfectionist, knowing that your husband or wife is expressing love through criticism might not be enough to ward off feelings of discouragement and resentment; it can be awfully wearing to feel that nothing is or ever will be good enough. So you might try confronting it head-on. Phrases like, "This isn't perfect, but . . .," can halt the flow of suggestions because it acknowledges the real problem the perfectionist perceives. You can even respond with a mischievous grin and, "Do you have any other criticisms?" The humor is important, because it helps diffuse the negative feelings that can arise in both of you.

"I Did It for You"

Perpetual pleasers are such good-hearted souls. They're always going out of their way to do things they think will make you happy, generous to a fault with their time, attention, and energy. But even though you know this is their way of showing how much they love you, sometimes you wish they just would stop it already.

Part of the problem is that pleasers get their feelings hurt if you aren't pleased with what they do; to them, it feels like you're rejecting their love. So, to avoid that kind of misunderstanding, you feel obligated to express pleasure, even when you don't really feel it. Then you feel pressured to do something to please them, and you feel guilty if you don't do it. And sometimes you get annoyed, even hurt, because they just assumed they knew what would please you without bothering to get your input. Eventually, you may just feel like withdrawing because the give-and-take of your relationship is out of whack: Your pleaser partner does all the giving, and all you're allowed to do is take.

What to do about it

If you are the perpetual pleaser in your relationship, you might not be seeing your spouse as an equal, especially if you're the one who is always giving. To give yourself a different perspective, write down your spouse's greatest strengths—the qualities you admire and find attractive. Focusing on your partner's strengths helps you back away from the compulsion to always be "doing" for him or her, because it forces you to see your partner as an equal.

If you're married to a perpetual pleaser, you can redirect his or her energies into things that really will please you by saying, "Please," as in, "Please wait to make the dinner reservations until I get hold of the sitter," or, "Please help me pick out a new paint color for the living room."

"I Bought You This"

Most of us consider gift-giving an expression of affection, but, for some people, it's the only way they regularly express love. And that can cause problems because the recipient may feel that the giver is trying to buy his or her love. Rather than feeling valued, the recipient actually may feel unloved, because the gift seems like a substitute for genuine affection.

Chronic gift-givers often feel unlovable themselves; on some level, they believe other people will like them only as long as they can continue to provide some tangible benefit, hence the gifts. When the recipient rejects the gift or seems less than ecstatic about it, the giver immediately feels insecure about the relationship, because rejecting the gift is the same as rejecting the giver.

What to do about it

If you're the gift-giver, challenge yourself to find other ways to express your love for your spouse. Believe it or not, sometimes a simple hug really does mean more than a dozen roses, and sometimes the best gift you can give is your attention.

If you're married to a gift-giver, the challenge for you is convincing your spouse that your love is not dependent on the things he or she can buy for you. You can acknowledge your spouse's deep-rooted doubts and still convey what you want by saying, "This may be hard for you to believe, but I'd rather have a quiet dinner with you at home than a night at a fancy restaurant."

Kicking Bad Habits

Marriage may promote good health because each of you encourages the other to avoid or change the things that contribute to poor health, such as smoking, excessive drinking, and lack of exercise. On the other hand, these bad habits—especially when they rise to the level of addiction—can sabotage a happy relationship because they get in the way of allowing you to enjoy life together.

The Nature of Addiction

An addiction is nothing more than an artificial way to feel good, and its roots stretch back to our childhood, usually around age six. This is when an adult, uncomfortable in seeing us feel bad and unable to alter whatever it was that was making us feel bad, tried to cheer us up with something else—cookies and milk, or a trip to the toy store, or anything that would take our minds off our troubles. The distraction usually was offered with, "Let's do this. It will make you feel better."

Well-intentioned as they were, these efforts to make us feel better led us to form two conclusions that few of us are aware of as adults but that can have a profound impact on our behavior. First, we learned that feeling bad is intolerable because the grown-ups couldn't tolerate it. And, second, we learned that there must be something out there somewhere that will make us feel good. If these conclusions have been reinforced over the course of our lives, we will continue to seek out a metaphorical "milk and cookies" to make us feel better when we're feeling bad.

. . . .

When Is It OK to Feel Bad?

Many of us unwittingly reinforce the idea that feeling bad is not OK by trying to cheer up our partners whenever they display the slightest bit of stress, disgruntlement, fatigue or unhappiness. Some of us do this because we want to "fix" a bad situation; some of us do it because we're highly sensitive to any kind of tension; some of us feel obliged to "rescue" our spouse from his or her bad feelings. One way to break the cycle is to train yourself to acknowledge bad feelings without trying to fix them, cover them up, or ignore them—for your spouse or for yourself. Feeling bad occasionally is part of the natural rhythm of life. Accept those times for what they are, and then get back to enjoying life together.

As adults, we have lots of substitutes for the six-year-old's milk and cookies, some of the most common being:

- Alcohol
- Drugs (prescription and illicit)
- "Comfort" food (including everything from ice cream and chocolate to mashed potatoes and gravy)
- Shopping
- Gambling
- Sex
- Risks

Most of us reach for these things (or whatever else helps us feel better) occasionally when our feeling bad gets to be too much for us. No one would argue that using one of these artificial mood-boosters to get over a hump or snap us out of an abnormally long funk is reasonable once in a while. But issues arise when we reach for these things at the first sign of trouble, or when we use these things as preventive measures to avoid ever feeling bad under any circumstances.

Getting Past the Addiction

Addictions are tough things to overcome, and many require professional counseling or even medical intervention to treat successfully. But you can start by changing your perspective on things. The first step is understanding that your addiction is an attempt to feel good. Knowing that, you can make a conscious choice to find natural ways to feel good by finding things to enjoy in everyday life—a favorite song, a conversation, even something as simple as the weather or the birds outside. Finally, you can decide to accept that you're going to feel bad once in a while, and you can choose to tolerate those times rather than trying to avoid or evade them.

If your spouse is fighting an addiction, you can encourage him or her by verbally enjoying your environment. Notice we did not say "encourage him or her to quit the addiction." Nagging doesn't work—never has, never will. At best, you will only succeed in forcing your spouse to hide the addiction from you; at worst, you'll compound the bad feelings that sparked the addiction in the first place. But by saying things like, "I love that view," or, "I like this chair," you direct your partner's attention to enjoying life. There's another benefit to this, too: When you say out loud what you like, you send a subliminal message to your partner that says, "I like you." And who doesn't feel better knowing someone likes them?

The Smoking Addiction

Smoking is a terrifically difficult habit to break, and it may be because this particular addiction was formed differently from the ones we've already discussed. Most smokers began smoking with their friends at a time when friends were vitally important—often in the middle school or high school years—so smoking became associated with pleasant social interaction. As smokers grow up, the act of smoking triggers the feelings attached to those memories, making the smoker feel calmer, more comfortable, and less isolated.

Most smokers who quit try several times before they finally succeed, and many of them get help from their doctors in the form of nicotine replacements, antidepressants, or other medications to ease the physical symptoms of withdrawal. Even so, the rate of smokers who are able to quit and are still tobacco-free after a year is discouraging, and experts agree that the most important component in successfully quitting is your own desire to become a nonsmoker.

Even those who are successful in quitting most likely will suffer a relapse. This usually happens about three weeks after the initial quit date; the smoker feels an almost overpowering urge to light up again and will find ways to justify going back to smoking. He or she may even indulge in "just one," which may lead to full-blown addiction again. Partners of those who are trying to quit smoking can help the smoker get through the relapse by providing emotional support—again, not nagging, but acknowledging the difficulty of the task and encouraging the spouse not to give up. For many smokers, the relapse may signal the end of one of numerous attempts to quit; for others, these powerful urges will dissipate in a day or two and the addiction will be conquered.

Promoting Good Habits

In addition to providing support for breaking bad habits, married couples tend to help each other develop good habits that contribute to longer, healthier lives. The one area where the married don't do as well as singles is in the area of weight control; research shows married people tend to be heavier. That said, however, couples can provide vital encouragement to each other when it comes to weight loss, exercise, and other healthy behaviors—like getting regular check-ups and making sure you follow doctor's orders when it comes to things like controlling high blood pressure or diabetes.

● ●

What's Your Fitness IQ?

"Insight 2007," a survey conducted for *Cooking Light* magazine by GfK Roper Public Affairs and Media, showed that less than half of Americans know how much physical activity it takes to burn off a pound of unwanted weight (you have to burn 3,500 calories more than you consume), and only slightly more than one in ten were aware that the USDA recommends thirty minutes of physical activity each day. Still, we do know we need to move more: Although only 6 percent of us get thirty minutes of exercise a day, a third of us regularly park farther away from the entrance to our destination and more than 40 percent of us take the stairs rather than the elevator in order to get in more walking.

In fact, encouragement may do more to help your partner's health than you realize. In a recent study, two Harvard researchers tested the theory that you can "think" yourself fit. Working with hotel maids, they first gave all the volunteers a standard physical exam. Then they divided the group in half and told one group that their daily activities—making beds, vacuuming, cleaning bathrooms, and so on—qualified as exercise and told them about the health benefits of exercise. The other group didn't get any information about the health benefits of their work activities and wasn't told that their activities counted as exercise. A month later, the researchers gave each of the maids another physical; those in the first group had lower blood pressure, had lost weight, and thought of themselves as healthier, while the maids in the second group experienced none of these benefits.

We don't know how much influence positive thinking has over our physical health, but the Harvard experiment indicates that it has a lot more than we're accustomed to believe; the maids didn't change their behavior during the experiment, only the way they thought about their behavior. So it's not so far-fetched to think you can improve your own and your spouse's health by thinking more positively about your (and your spouse's) behavior. By the same token, it's possible that nagging and criticizing can actually harm your (or your spouse's) health, because you end up thinking negatively about your behavior.

Instead of thinking about how little exercise you get, for instance, try thinking about how much you get just doing chores around the house, and when your spouse complains about not having time to exercise, point out the things he or she does daily that contribute to his or her good health. Doing laundry involves bending, stretching, and lifting, for example. When you do yard work or wash the car or walk to the mailbox and back—that's exercise, and just thinking of it that way can be enough to improve your overall health.

. . . .

A Calorie by Any Other Name . . .

Despite what the latest fad diets and exercise gurus may claim, there is mounting evidence that eating fewer calories and burning more through exercise are equally effective in losing weight, because a calorie is a calorie, whether it's eaten in a salad or a piece of pie and whether it's burned off by a five-mile run or rearranging the living room furniture. As reported in the Journal of Clinical Endocrinology and Metabolism, researchers have shown there is no way to target specific areas of fat deposits, and dieting without exercise apparently does not lead to a loss of muscle mass. Finally, adding muscle mass does not boost your metabolism. So, if you want to shed unwanted pounds, the best advice still is what your mother always told you: Eat less and move more.

A Few Things to Watch

It would be impossible to cover every possible health concern in this book, or to offer a definitive list of things you and your spouse should keep an eye on to make sure you stay healthy. There are countless other resources for such information, starting with your own doctor. But there are a few potential problem areas that may indicate something more serious and that few people are aware of.

Catch Up on Your Sleep

Problems sleeping can indicate other potentially serious health issues, or even lead to such problems. According to a study by Brigham and Women's Hospital in Boston, women especially need to make sure they get enough sleep: Those who get fewer than five hours a night have a higher risk, by almost a third, of developing heart disease than those who get a full eight hours.

Insufficient sleep also is believed to contribute to problems with blood pressure, hormone, and blood sugar levels.

Snoring can be another indicator of serious health problems. Aside from the strain it can create in your relationship—particularly if one partner is the snorer and the other loses sleep from the snoring—those harsh rasps, whistles, and rattles can indicate anything from a deviated septum (the cartilage that separates the nostrils) to high blood pressure, or even the potentially life-threatening condition of sleep apnea, where the sufferer actually stops breathing for seconds at a time.

Counselors recommend against couples sleeping in separate rooms because of snoring, partly because, for many couples, bed-time is the only chance they have during the day to talk quietly and privately. Another reason to stay together is so you can monitor each other; very often, the snorer is unaware of his or her sleep patterns, and an alert spouse can spot signs that warrant a visit to the doctor.

Pay Attention to Your Sex Life

The patterns of your sex life will change over the course of your relationship as the demands of your lives change. But unexplained lapses in frequency or libido, even impotence, could signal an underlying health issue like depression or heart disease. Other conditions, such as kidney failure, diabetes, and hormonal imbalances, also can interfere with your sex drive.

Don't run away with the idea that your partner has heart problems or a chronic disease just because he or she wasn't in the mood last night. But if you or your partner just don't seem to have any interest in making love, and if this state of affairs persists even after other potential causes—a rush of deadlines at work or stress over a child's performance in school, say—have exhausted themselves, it might be time to talk with your doctor.

Be Health-Literate

It doesn't matter how often you go to the doctor if you don't understand what he or she is telling you. This isn't a function of education, income, or any other demographic factor: The U.S. Surgeon General reported in 2006 that more than ninety million American adults do not understand the language most doctors use to inform us about our health. That lack of understanding makes patients less likely to use their prescription medications properly, less likely to engage in preventive health care measures like screening tests and wellness exams, more likely to be hospitalized, and, in fact, more likely to die.

You and your spouse can help each other become more health-literate by asking questions of your doctor whenever he or she says something you don't understand. Repeat his or her instructions to make sure they're clear and you know how to take prescribed medications, etc. If it helps, take notes while you're in the doctor's office, and, if you still find you don't always understand the medical lingo, ask your spouse to accompany you to your doctor's visits. Sometimes just having your partner there will calm your anxieties and let you focus on what the doctor is saying.

When you took your vows, you promised to love and cherish each other for richer or poorer, in sickness and in health. By nurturing the bond between you and providing the support each of you needs, you can help each other ensure that you'll spend more time together in health.

1. Hold hands, share bear hugs, and cuddle on the couch.
2. Sleep together in the same bed every night.

3. Find ways to acknowledge and appreciate each other that suit your personality types.
4. Encourage your spouse to give up unhealthy habits, such as smoking; do not nag.
5. Spend time together participating in healthy activities: take walks, play tennis, etc.
6. Encourage one another to eat well, exercise, and get regular medical and dental check-ups.
7. Act as each other's advocate when dealing with health issues and health care professionals.

CHAPTER 11

The Confidence Factor

One of the blurriest lines couples must learn to walk is the one between healthy reliance on each other and clinginess. The former encourages each partner to explore interests independently while providing a "safe harbor" at home. The latter can end up smothering a marriage.

There are, certainly, different kinds of dependency, as well as different degrees. Psychologists at the University of Wisconsin have identified three kinds of what they call "dependent behavior patterns": submissiveness, in which the person crumbles immediately to the will of others; exploitability, in which the person is easily led because he or she doesn't want to offend; and love dependency, in which the person longs for social contact. Love dependency is at the core of a healthy marriage. It is what urges us to come home and tell our spouse what happened today, to make plans to spend time together, to enjoy quiet moments with each other. This kind of dependency isn't always healthy, though. Sometimes it crosses the line into unhealthy neediness.

Defining Healthy Dependence

It seems like the whole of human existence is a tug of war between dependence and independence. We start our lives completely dependent on others for our basic well-being, and the instant we gain some measure of independence—like being able to walk or open doors—somebody comes along and puts gates up in front of the stairs and those little childproof things on the bathroom cupboards. Fast-forward ten or fifteen years, and suddenly the same people who did everything for us when we were babies now get mad at us when we ask them to do things for us instead of doing them ourselves. We have to learn to be independent, they tell us, to stand on our own two feet and go out into the world able to take care of ourselves. So, fine, we learn the skills we need to take care of ourselves, and nearly as soon as we get comfortable being on our own, people start demanding that we find a nice boy or girl to settle down with. Small wonder we have a hard time distinguishing between annoyingly needy and healthily dependent.

. . . .

Dependency Leads to Success?

A recent study of forty-eight students at Gettysburg College in Pennsylvania found that those who scored high on dependency tests had better grades than those who tested more independent. Researchers think more dependent people are more likely to seek help from others than the fiercely self-sufficient, and that willingness to ask for assistance may translate into a higher degree of success—at least in the classroom.

Healthy dependence—what some call *interdependence*—is characterized by three things: a relationship between equals; an atmosphere that fosters each partner's self-confidence; and affirmation of each other's strengths.

Love Between Equals

Love is like water. It flows on a level plane—have you ever spilled something on the table?—and it flows downhill, but it doesn't flow uphill. In an unequal relationship, one partner is above the other, and only the one on the higher plane is capable of love. The one on the lower plane may well need the other, but need is not the same as love. Love occurs between equals.

That's not to say that people who love each other don't also need each other. But in a well-balanced relationship, the need is mutual and minimal. Consider the difference in your relationship with your spouse versus your relationship with your child. Parents love their children, but they don't need them in the same way children need their parents. The need isn't mutual, and it isn't minimal, at least not until the children grow up and are able to relate with their parents as adults. With your spouse, though, the need is mutual. You rely on your spouse to do his or her part to make your life together what you want it to be, and he or she relies on you in the same way. The need also is minimal: You could, if you had to, survive and even thrive again on your own.

Some adults confuse being needed with being loved. Over the past several decades, this has often been an issue for men, whose traditional role as the family provider has eroded as more women have entered the workforce and started earning higher salaries. By the same token, women who concentrated on the homemaking skills our grandmothers honed so sharply sometimes feel obsolete when confronted with men who are not only capable of cooking a fine meal but who enjoy doing it. If women no longer need men to bring home the bacon, and men no longer need women to fry it up—well, what's to keep us together? It can be frightening to let go of the tether of need.

It also can be liberating, and a tremendous ego boost. If your partner doesn't need to stay with you to get by, that means he or she *wants* to be with you. It means he or she has chosen to stay with you. And, since you also have chosen to be with your partner, it is the freedom of choice that really bonds you to each other. Out of all the people in the world, your spouse chooses to be with you. How can that not make you feel good?

Building Self-Confidence

Knowing that you and your partner are together because you choose to be is good for your sense of self. A healthy relationship is also good for your self-confidence—the ability to turn problems into challenges. Problems are scary things; they make us want to run and hide, and we need others to make them go away. Challenges enliven us, encourage us to dig into ourselves and discover our own capabilities; they make us strong.

We Learn Fear by Watching Others

You don't have to personally experience fear to feel the effects of it, researchers have learned. The part of the brain that responds when we experience a painful or frightening event—the amygdala—also leaps into action when we simply witness someone else's fear. And we don't even have to witness real fear; the visceral responses we have to horror movies and suspense novels prove that. Researchers think this may explain why some people develop phobias of things like snakes, spiders, perhaps even people of other races, regardless of whether they've ever had much personal experience with them. When it comes to your marriage, reactions to each other's fears might follow one of two patterns: One might pick up on the other's fear and become frightened, or one might become braver to prove that the other's fears are groundless or overblown.

Spouses help each other build self-confidence by offering each other unconditional love. That doesn't mean you're always going to be happy with each other's behavior. But it does mean both of you know that the other's love is not conditioned upon external factors, like whether you get the promotion you were seeking or whether your new business succeeds. Unconditional love tells you that your spouse will love you even if you don't make as much money as someone else, even if you make a mistake, even if an idea of yours doesn't work out. It takes performance anxiety out of the relationship and replaces it with safety, allowing you to stretch, grow, and learn the things that, in turn, make you stronger.

Drawing on Each Other's Strengths

Healthy interdependence means that you and your spouse can take advantage of each other's strengths and use those strengths to enrich your own experience. It's not unlike cross-breeding varieties of corn. One type of corn may excel at fighting off pests, while another is good at thriving in dry conditions. Combine the two, and you get the strengths of each in one new variety of corn. In marriage, the two of you have combined your strengths to make a new unit. Each of you has willingly set aside some of your individual independence in order to be enriched by the other.

To achieve this takes commitment, a genuine desire to do good for each other, and a voluntary cession of some of the freedoms you enjoyed when you were single. You can no longer pack up and move across the country at a whim, for example; your lives are intertwined, and what one does affects the other, for good or bad. Much depends on how well the two of you have fortified your relationship with the things that nourish you both.

Trust

Trust is a sense of security, the implicit knowledge that neither of you wants to intentionally hurt the other. Of course, there will be times when you inadvertently cause pain; that's the nature of all relationships. But the intent is as important as the actual hurt. We cannot trust those whom we suspect of being willing to harm us, physically or emotionally.

Trust also allows us to let our spouses explore their own interests without feeling threatened. Your wife's involvement in the local library doesn't represent competition for her attention. Neither does your husband's membership in the local American Legion. With trust, neither of you feels the need to restrict the other's interests. And because you aren't worried about competing for your partner's attention, you can enjoy the added dimensions your partner's outside interests bring to your marriage.

Responsibility

There's the sense of responsibility toward your spouse that keeps you from staying out all night with the girls or spending the mortgage money on a new home theater system. But there's also a sense of responsibility for your spouse's well-being, particularly his or her emotional well-being. The idea that love means never having to say you're sorry is a Hollywood myth. Trust cannot survive in a relationship where partners don't recognize and apologize when they do hurt each other, even unintentionally.

We're not saying it's your fault if your spouse is unhappy, or vice versa. In a healthy relationship, though, each partner holds the other's well-being in high regard. You want your spouse to be happy, and you do what you can to make your spouse feel loved. And when you inadvertently hurt your spouse by being thoughtless or inconsiderate—as we all do from time to time—your regard for your spouse leads you to apologize, to do what you can to heal or at least assuage the hurt you've caused, and to correct the behavior that led to the hurt.

Accepting the Flaws

The flip side of the responsibility coin is the willingness to forgive our spouses. Holding grudges does no one any good; such negativity hurts us physically and can mortally wound our relationships. A healthy marriage is one in which transgressions are acknowledged and forgiven so that both of you can get on with the rest of your lives together. In combination with trust and your sense of responsibility toward each other, the mistakes that we all make occasionally can evaporate like dew off the grass, never festering long enough to damage the roots.

Sometimes, especially at the height of our irritation, it's hard not to see our spouse's flaws to the exclusion of all else. But most flaws are minor, outweighed by the traits we admire—the things we were drawn to from the beginning. You don't want your spouse to demand or expect perfection from you; the pressure would be too great. Give yourself permission, then, to love your spouse even though he or she isn't perfect, and that will help you get over the times when his or her flawed humanity gets the upper hand.

The Two Sides of Encouragement

Couples encourage each other to do well by taking an interest in each other's activities, expressing confidence in each other's abilities, and providing emotional support when it's needed. As we discussed in Chapter 3, our spouses are our reality checks, reminding us of our strengths when we can't see them and taming our fears when we allow them to grow out of proportion. But sometimes our well-meant attempts at encouragement end up having the opposite effect. Instead of building our partner's self-confidence, we can actually undermine it.

Just as some people seem to need a lot of encouragement, others seem to need to offer encouragement. To fulfill this need, they pay attention to their partners' fears, weaknesses, and failures. They tend to ignore successes because success doesn't require encouragement. As a result, weaknesses get reinforced and strengths atrophy, in the same way that one plant given constant attention will blossom while a neglected plant will die.

The difference between helpful encouragement and the not-so-helpful kind lies in whether we focus on our partners' abilities or on faith that "everything will be OK." Encouragement that focuses on our partners is affirmation of their capability. Encouragement that focuses on faith in the future is mere assurance to allay fears. It's the difference between telling your spouse, "You are capable," and, "It will all work out."

See how you react to the following sentences:

- It's going to turn out OK.
- People will be impressed.
- You are needed.
- People will depend on you.
- You'll be accepted.

For most of us, these phrases don't inspire confidence; they inspire doubt. Even if we don't say it out loud, our initial reaction when someone says any of these things to us is, "Really?" If we're feeling particularly pessimistic, we may reject the intended reassurance altogether, thinking, if not saying, "How do you know?" or "I don't think so."

Now read the sentences below and see if your reaction is different.

- You know how to do things right.
- You can find out how to do things.
- You're able to do what is necessary.
- You're able to find new ways of doing things.
- You're able to work hard to get things done.

These statements make us reflect on our own abilities and agree or disagree. They affirm our strengths by reminding us of what we know and what we're capable of. Very rarely will we disagree with such statements, because immediately we'll draw on something in our experience that supports the statement.

. . . .

Fear May Be Linked to Cancer

University of Chicago scientists recently performed a study that showed a striking correlation between fearfulness and cancer in lab rats. Previous studies had found that adventurous male rats had longer life spans. For the more recent study, the researchers used female rats from breeds that commonly develop certain types of cancer and, when the rats were 20 days old, measured how far they were willing to explore a safe but unfamiliar environment. By the time the rats reached middle age, at about thirteen months, four out of five of the timid rats had developed cancer, compared with fewer than four in ten of the more courageous rats. Whether these findings will translate to humans is uncertain, but one of the researchers said it may be time for human cancer research to look at how fear might affect hormones and other biological factors associated with certain types of cancer.

Empowering Your Partner

Using affirmations gives your spouse permission to use his or her strengths to achieve goals. It's a critical part of communication in any relationship, and particularly in marriage, because we look to our spouses first to provide effective encouragement.

When I was starting my counseling practice, I needed encouragement from my wife and from others. I was scared at the prospect of running my own practice. I wasn't sure it would work, and I wasn't sure how to make it work. Kathy told me I did good counseling—affirming my abilities. The editor of the local newspaper advised me not to expect clients to flock to my office just because I hung out a shingle, and he gave me some pointers on how to promote my practice—again, affirming what I could do and warning me against magical expectations. Others encouraged me by telling me the community needed what I wanted to offer.

If these people had simply told me everything was going to work out OK, I would have been skeptical at best, overcome with self-doubt at worst. Encouragement that focused on what I could do was empowering because it kept me centered in reality and prompted me to be proactive in accomplishing what I wanted to do.

Valuing Time Apart

It might seem counterintuitive, but couples who spend every available moment together are less likely to develop a strong and lasting bond than couples who spend some time away from each other. Part of the reason for this is that, no matter how close we are to our spouses, it's impossible for one person to meet all of our social, intellectual, or emotional needs. Sometimes guys just need to hang out with other guys, and gals need to talk with other gals. Time away from each other also allows us to process what we know about each other; when we're parked in each other's back pockets all the time, we never get a chance to digest the other's nonverbal communication, reactions to stress, and so on.

Interaction with other people inevitably gives us material for comparison, which many of us do without even being conscious of it. How many times have you come home from a difficult day at work, for instance, and told your spouse you don't know how your boss's wife manages to put up with him? Observing and interacting with other people can remind us of what we like and appreciate about our spouses—always a good thing. If we are never around other people, though, it's easy to lose sight of those good qualities, and less desirable qualities can get blown out of proportion—never a good thing.

Finally, time apart gives each of us the space we need to tend to our sense of self. At home, we may find it hard to escape the labels of cook, cleaner, launderer, chauffeur, and personal shopper. With our spouses, our identities are naturally entwined with theirs; we're so-and-so's wife or husband and what's-her-name's parent. And while we fill all these roles with pride, they don't do complete justice to our sense of self. Time away from the roles associated with our marriage and our home is an essential tool in maintaining a well-rounded sense of self.

The Three Areas of Relating

All of us have to relate to ourselves, to others, and to life in general. And all three of these relating requirements come with their own blocks and hazards. In relating to ourselves, the issue is loving ourselves. As children, we were told not to be selfish; often we were told to count our blessings because other children were not as fortunate as we were. The message we took away was, "Don't love yourself. Love others." And that becomes a burden that follows us into adulthood.

When it comes to relating to others, the real issue is being able to agree with someone else; we can't relate to anybody if we can't agree with them. As children, we were forced to agree with adults, whether we really agreed or not. So now we have a natural resistance to agreeing.

Finally, relating to life can pose a problem because, all our lives, we've been subjected to limits in our enjoyment of life, often by being told that once we made a choice, we were stuck with it. So the issue in adulthood is really about freedom—being able to enjoy life on our own terms, and being able to change our minds.

If any (or all) of these strike a chord with you, here's what we want you to do. Write these messages to yourself on a piece of paper and post them on the refrigerator, the bathroom mirror, your home computer, or anywhere else where you'll see them often:

- Forget making yourself love yourself; just let yourself love yourself.
- Forget making yourself agree; just let yourself agree.
- Forget making yourself be free; just let yourself be free.

These simple reminders will help you bring all three areas of relating into balance, allowing you to feel good about yourself, connected to other people, and free to enjoy life. And, after all, what else is there?

Walking That Blurry Line

Finding the perfect balance between overdependence and no dependence at all is a challenge at the best of times. Truth be told, if you're like most couples, the moments when you and your spouse achieve it will be temporary, lasting only until something unexpected comes along to knock you toward one extreme or the other. There will be times when your spouse will have to lean on you more heavily, and other times when you'll be the one who needs to lean. The knack lies in being able to stop leaning when the need is no longer there—to avoid falling into a habit where one of you feels overburdened and the other feels helpless.

It's OK to be the rescuer sometimes, and it's OK to need rescuing sometimes. But, to get back to a healthy interdependence, the goal of both rescuer and rescued must be restoring an equal footing.

1. Acknowledge that out of all of the people in the world, you have chosen one another.
2. Love each other unconditionally.
3. Acknowledge each other's strengths and weaknesses— and how yours complement his, and vice versa.
4. Trust each other to do the right thing.
5. Learn to say you are sorry—and mean it.
6. Practice tolerance—and forgiveness.
7. Bolster each other's self-esteem.
8. Empower each other to achieve goals and overcome obstacles.
9. Give each other room to spend time apart, whether alone or with friends and family.

CHAPTER 12

Adjusting to the Empty Nest

The day you've been working toward for years is finally here. Your children are grown and ready to go out into the world on their own, independent, strong, adventurous, and determined. You watch them go with a confusing welter of emotion—part pride, part worry, part delight. You have been eagerly awaiting and anxiously dreading this moment, and now that it's here . . . well, now what?

For many couples, the "empty nest" is a wonderful time. In fact, in happiness surveys, empty nesters are happier than parents whose children haven't grown up yet; one researcher said the chief symptom of the empty nest seems to be "more smiles." You have the privacy you've lacked for at least eighteen years. You don't have to find a babysitter or wait up on prom night. Your grocery bill and electric bill drop back to manageable levels. Your phone isn't constantly tied up, you can watch what you want to watch on television, and you can keep cash in your wallet for days, even weeks at a time. Best of all, you and your spouse are able to concentrate on each other again without the distractions of children. You can get back to being a couple, just as you were before you started your family.

Unfortunately, this happy picture is just a fantasy for lots of couples. Without the children at home to interact with or discuss, some spouses find they have nothing to say to each other.

Couples who have let resentments pile up over the years as they have attended to the immediate needs of the family find themselves bubbling over with anger toward each other. The social networks that consisted primarily of the parents of other children may disintegrate, having nothing to sustain them beyond soccer games or youth groups.

In short, this can be a crisis time for your marriage. While overall divorce rates have remained flat over the past twenty years, the rate of divorce for couples married thirty or more years actually has increased. The combination of changing parental roles and changing priorities for each spouse can be too much for a marriage to bear, particularly if the bond between you has been allowed to languish in the background in deference to all the other demands on your time and energy.

The Midlife Shift

Men and women tend to be at opposite ends of the spectrum at opposing times of life. During the first two decades of adulthood, men tend to focus their energies on building their careers, making money, and pursuing the achievements that will help them advance in their chosen fields. Women tend to be more relationship-focused in these years, concentrating their energies on providing the emotional support their husbands and children need in order to thrive. Oftentimes, if they work outside the home, it's primarily to provide extra income; the family still occupies the top spot on their list of priorities.

After the first twenty years, men and women swap priorities. Men become more interested in relationships than in their careers, and women begin to focus less on the needs of others and more on their own wants and needs. Problems arise when couples don't recognize or understand the shift in each other's priorities.

From the husband's perspective, his wife is behaving irrationally. For years she has complained that all he ever thought about was work. She has pleaded with him to spend more time with her and the kids. She has argued with him about the relative importance of a business meeting compared with their daughter's starring role in the school play. And now that he is ready to see things her way, to concentrate on spending time with her and reacquainting himself with the things in life that really matter, she's off gallivanting to college classes or her job or her volunteer work. It's frustrating. What does she want from him?

The wife, meanwhile, feels that her husband just doesn't get it. For years she listened to him vent about his boss and worry about money. She was the one who took the kids to doctor's appointments and dentist appointments. She was the one who did most of the household errands and most of the household chores. She put off doing what she would have liked to do because the family's needs came first, and she was happy to do it. But now the kids are gone, he's well-established in his career, and it's her turn to do the things she wants to do. It's frustrating. Does he expect her to give up this phase of life, too?

This scenario may resonate for fewer couples today than it did a generation ago. More men and women are delaying marriage and having children to complete their educations and concentrate on their careers, and this pattern may alleviate much of the potential discomfort of the midlife transition because the priorities of each spouse are in closer alignment throughout. But for couples who identify with the preceding two paragraphs, the midlife transition is a frightening and dangerous time.

A New Way to Relate

One of the biggest challenges for empty-nest couples is figuring out how to relate to each other as individual adults instead of as parents. Like any habit, this one is difficult to break and might even lead to a period where one of you is treating the other like a child. On the other hand, if you try to relate to each other the way you did when you were newlyweds, you're likely to feel just as uncomfortable. The fact is that, just like every other stage of life, you're in a situation that neither of you has experienced before, and you're going to have to redefine normal. The good news is that this redefining process can be a lot of fun and richly rewarding for both of you.

There's more good news: You already know how to do this. The process is the same as it was during your courtship—talking, doing things together, sharing your sense of humor, and building on your talks and activities to become emotional intimates again. The difference now is that you have a shared history to build on.

Talking to each other

Men who expect their relationship with their wives to consist mainly of hugs and kisses and long, soulful conversations on the sofa in front of the fire are apt to be disappointed. But men who take an interest in their wives' activities may well learn new dimensions of their partners' personalities. When she wants to talk about her day at work or what she's learning in the classes she's taking or the goals her volunteer group has set, she's letting you in on an important part of her life. She is, in fact, relating to you as a friend and confidant. Treating her priorities as irrelevant closes off the ability to relate to her and puts her on the defensive.

Women may be a little apprehensive about sharing these things with their husbands, for fear that he will be dismissive or, even worse, will attempt to take over these aspects of her life, telling her what to do and how to do it. She may come to feel as protective of her activities as she once felt of the children, and she may pull back from sharing information with him as part of her protectiveness.

Doing things together

It is just as important in this phase of your marriage to spend time together doing things as it is during any other phase. Dating—that is, getting away from home together—reminds you of each other's fun qualities, which too often can be overlooked amid the pressures of maintaining the household. Whether it's with a group or just the two of you, your commitment to "date night" should be just as inviolable when the kids are away at college as it was when they were in preschool. (Chapter 6 explores ways to keep dating for a lifetime.)

Participation is the key to pleasure. The people who enjoy life the most are the ones who do things—not those who sit idly by and watch or wait for things to happen. Gardening is more enjoyable than watching a gardening show on TV. Taking a weekend trip is more fun than waiting for the perfect time to take it. If you and your spouse find yourselves waiting and watching more than doing, figure out a way to participate more. One way to do this is to discuss the circumstances and attitudes that might be holding you back. It's common to think you can't or shouldn't take that weekend trip, for instance, if you're trying to catch up on your retirement savings. And if things are really bad, we tend to believe it isn't possible—or even morally right—to enjoy ourselves. If you're stuck in this way of thinking, remember how people pitched in to help in the aftermath of Hurricane Katrina, or the 2004 Asian tsunami, or any of dozens of natural disasters. There is a sense of satisfaction and even joy that comes from doing what you can, even if it isn't much. Even better, you don't have to wait for a disaster to enjoy doing something; you can find ways to enjoy doing things no matter what your situation may be. An added bonus: Not only do you get pleasure from the doing, you get another boost of pleasure later on by remembering something you did.

Enjoying a laugh together

Tension and pressure can make us less receptive to humor from others as well as less inclined to use humor ourselves. You might find that sharing humor comes more easily now that you don't have to worry about the children in the same way. Talking and doing things together should naturally lead to sharing humor, and you might find yourself reveling in a rediscovered sense of feeling relaxed and comfortable with your spouse.

Stubbornness, Good and Bad

One of the obstacles to enjoying this new phase of marriage is our innate stubbornness. Stubbornness is really resistance to change, and we all have it to some degree. Like so many of our adult traits, this one stretches from our pasts, when we were children and had change forced upon us. Change that was not of our choosing happened to us virtually from birth and virtually every day of our young lives, starting perhaps with the change in our routine when Mom went back to work and dropped us off at daycare or with a sitter. When we were old enough to walk, adults starting changing the rules about where and how and when we could walk ourselves; sometimes they put us in a stroller when we wanted to walk, and other times they refused to carry us when we didn't want to walk. Later on, we had to change our daily routines to fit school in. At the end of summer, we had to go to bed earlier, even though it was still light out and we still had plenty of play in us. We got new teachers every year at school whether we liked it or not, and then they started giving us different teachers for every subject, again without consulting us. Our bodies starting changing and there was nothing we could do about it. We graduated from high school and our friends moved away and we had to walk into a new situation again, at school or at work. Growing up consisted pretty much of accommodating the changes that other people (or biology) dictated.

You'd think that, what with all this experience, we'd be pretty immune to the discomfort of change by now, adopting a philosophical, go-with-the-flow kind of attitude and taking life as it comes. Some lucky people can do that, and they seem to weather the vicissitudes of life pretty well. For the rest of us, though, change—especially change that we haven't planned for or had a hand in—makes us dig in our heels like a dog that doesn't want to go for a walk. Even when resistance is futile (and it usually is), we still cling stubbornly to the way things have always been.

Sometimes stubbornness is a good thing. It allows us to resist unnecessary changes and even changes that might be harmful. But if it isn't balanced with a certain amount of flexibility, stubbornness can make us brittle. Instead of being strong enough to bend—flexible enough to go with the flow while still hanging on to the things that really matter and shouldn't change—we become stiff and vulnerable to breaking.

People who have a hard time adjusting to the changes in the empty nest can get around the harmful effects of stubbornness by telling themselves, "Forget making yourself change." This piece of self-talk turns change into something you can choose to do, rather than something you have to do. You can still be stubborn when you need to be, but you also can be flexible when it's appropriate. You can accept the changes in this stage of your marriage, since those changes aren't going to go away, and you can adapt while still protecting and building on the core strengths of your relationship.

Common Midlife Challenges

For most couples, the really difficult adjustment period lasts about six months after the last child leaves home. But some couples have to deal with more than just the unaccustomed quiet around the house. You may have aging parents to care for. You may be going through menopause, which can trigger its own physical and mental health issues. You may be worried about your preparations (or lack thereof) for retirement. You might even be worried that your child isn't ready to be off on his or her own.

Fortunately, talking about these challenges can help you cope with them. Sometimes just sharing your fears and worries is enough to take the sting out of them; saying them out loud to someone else strips them of much of the power they accumulate when they're isolated inside your own mind. Discussing these things with your spouse also reinforces your bond, allowing you to draw on each other's fortes and come up with solutions together. These challenges are opportunities for each of you to give strength, reassurance, and courage to the other.

Every Life Needs Fire Escapes

The fear of being trapped can keep us from doing what we want to do, so it's important to have a Plan B—a fire escape that will let us get to safety if we need to. Without fire escapes, we have to rely on things working out the way we planned, and since we rarely have total control over how things work out, that forced faith can be scary. What if you hate the new job you're considering taking? What if you discover that you don't really want to go back to school after all? If you don't have an alternative plan, you might end up avoiding taking the risks that would enhance your life. The same rule applies in your marriage after the kids have grown and moved away. You might not be willing to take a chance on a new direction if you don't have a fire escape available. Talking with your spouse about your hopes and fears can help you devise fire escapes that will protect what is most dear to you while still letting you explore new things.

Planning Ahead

You, your spouse, and your children benefit when you give yourself permission to envision the future. Talking with your children about their ideas for the future helps you gauge how well-prepared they are for the realities they'll encounter. It also gives you insight into their hopes, dreams, and aspirations, which will be very different at eighteen than they were at eight. This marks a seminal change in your relationship with your child, an opportunity for you to come to know and appreciate each other as adults. For the first time in your lives, you have the ability to enjoy each other on an equal footing.

You and your spouse can alleviate much of the normal discomfort that comes with the empty nest by planning for it, too. Talk about the things you've always wanted to do but couldn't because your energies and resources went into raising your family. If money were no object, what would you do? If time were unlimited, what would you do? When you were twenty, what was your dream job, your dream vacation, your dream home? Are those still your dreams, or have they changed?

Asking Advice

The reason support groups for things like cancer and widowhood and addiction are helpful is because everyone has a common frame of reference, even though their experiences may vary wildly. The same is true for the stages of your marriage. You probably won't get much empathy or useful advice about dealing with your empty nest from your childless friends or those whose children are still in grade school. Your best option is to talk to people who have been through it themselves. They may have insights or perspectives you and your spouse never would have thought of.

This period might also be a time for you to consider counseling to address unresolved issues. These might be related to your marriage or not. It's not uncommon for adults in this midlife phase to seek professional help, because very often they have put off dealing with the issues or suppressed them so they could do what they needed to do for their families. Sometimes attending counseling together is helpful; sometimes it's more helpful for spouses to have individual sessions.

Listening to Each Other

Listening is a skill that most people have to practice; it doesn't seem to come naturally to many of us, and it is an especially rare skill in marriage. The cacophony of careers, children, home life, and community life bombards us so that we become selectively deaf out of sheer self-preservation. Comparatively, much of our communication with our spouse is conducted at little more than a whisper, and therefore is too easily and too often ignored.

The value of listening lies in concentrating on what the other person is saying. Most of us don't do this automatically. About halfway through the other person's comments, we start thinking about what we're going to say next. As a result, we miss hearing at least half of what it is we intend to respond to. To make things even trickier, we all have different ways of not listening.

The interpreter

Some of us interrupt and respond to what we think the other person means instead of what he or she actually said. If the other person is talking about the mess in the kitchen, for instance, we may interpret it as an accusation and interrupt to defend ourselves, saying something like, "I haven't had time to unload the dishwasher yet." If we sound sufficiently defensive (and we often do), the other person may become irritated that we took offense when none was meant.

If you're inclined to not listen to your spouse this way, train yourself to ask for clarification before responding. You can even use humor to draw attention to a perceived criticism: "I was going to change into Super Housekeeper today, but my cape is in the laundry." If your spouse is the one who fails to listen by misinterpreting, you can snap him or her out of the habit by saying, "That's not what I mean. Pay attention to what I'm saying."

The yes man (or woman)

Some of us just agree with whatever someone says to us without thinking about whether we really agree or not. Those of us who do this are usually not very good at listening to ourselves; when someone asks us what we think or what we want, our stock reply is, "I don't know. What do you think (or want)?" It's very difficult to break out of this habit, because we don't want to offend anybody. The thing is, some people get annoyed with us precisely because we won't offer our own opinion, and then we feel doubly guilty because we offended them anyway.

If your spouse is the yes man or woman, you'll go gray waiting for him or her to change on his or her own. A better tactic is to give your spouse permission to disagree with you. Just saying, "You might not agree, but . . ." lets your spouse know that it's OK, even expected, for him or her to offer an opinion that doesn't jibe with yours.

The nit-picker

Some of us just seem to be waiting for a speaker to make a mistake so we can pounce on it. If our spouse says it's supposed to be a lovely day, we counter that the forecast on the radio called for afternoon showers. If our spouse likes a particular car model, we point out that a different model gets better gas mileage. If our spouse compliments our roast, we say we left it in too long and let it get dry. In short, our spouse can't win because we're only listening to the flaws and are deaf to everything else.

It's hard to break out of this pattern, but it can be done. You can hedge your bets: "I hope you're right about the weather, but I'll bring the umbrella anyway." You can make a rule for yourself that you must say at least one nice thing before you're allowed to make a criticism. When it comes to compliments, which can be the most difficult thing for the nit-picker not to criticize, the simplest solution is also the most graceful: Say "thank you," and then shut up. If you can't shut up, phrase your criticism in the form of a question, like, "You're sure the roast wasn't too dry?" When your spouse says no, it was fine, say, "Oh, I'm glad." And then shut up.

If your spouse is the nit-picker, you can often stop the criticism even before it begins by saying, "This may not be perfect, but . . ." Acknowledging imperfection at the beginning frees your spouse from being compelled to point it out for you.

The pleaser

Very similar in method to the interpreter, the pleaser tries to divine the intent behind what you're saying, but, of course, won't accept the intent at face value. If you say it's a nice day, for instance, the pleaser might wonder whether that means you want to go for a walk or take a leisurely drive, and he or she might start throwing out suggestions for enjoying the nice day before you even get a chance to finish your thought. Because the pleaser is so focused on intent, he or she very often misses the unambiguous meaning behind what you say. This is why this person may often fail to do things you've asked him or her to do. If you say, "Would you please take out the trash?" the pleaser almost automatically starts thinking, "Maybe I'm not doing enough around the house," or, "Do I have to be reminded like a child to do my chores?" You can see how this can lead to further miscommunication.

If you're the pleaser, it can be difficult to stop trying to read between the lines, and it may take quite a bit of practice to learn to focus on the actual content of the communication rather than what may (or may not) be hidden behind it. Self-talk in the form of, "I want to take people at their word," might help. If your spouse is a pleaser, the most effective way to get him or her to pay attention is to ask politely: "Please listen to me." The "please" lets your spouse know how he or she can please you (by listening).

The skeptic

The most pervasive aspects of the interpreter and the pleaser are combined in the skeptic, who never takes anything anybody says at face value and who is always trying to figure out what people really mean and comparing what they say now to what they've said in the past. This constant analyzing leads the skeptic to automatically distrust anything anyone says, even his or her nearest and dearest.

If you're a skeptic, it may be hard for you to believe that you can take your spouse at his or her word. You might feel like you're always waiting for the other shoe to drop, so you're always on the alert for the subtlest sign of betrayal or deception. Try asking yourself if it's OK for you to believe your spouse. When you can answer yes without hesitation, you'll be able to turn off the analyzing and focus on listening to what your spouse is saying.

If your spouse is a skeptic, the most effective way to get him or her to listen is to acknowledge this particular obstacle up front. "This may be hard for you to believe, but . . ." is a gentle but effective way to temporarily turn off the analysis. Sometimes, though, the skeptic may need a more forceful reminder. You can deliver this by saying, "Stop it! It's like this . . ." This breaks the skeptic out of his inner analysis and refocuses him on what you're saying.

Listening is one of those skills that can fade for lack of practice. Just as you might be a little wobbly on a bicycle if you haven't ridden one for years, your ability to really listen to your spouse might be a little rusty if you haven't had the time, energy, or inclination to do it for a while. Fortunately, just like riding a bike and countless other skills that enhance your relationship but that don't always get the attention they deserve, listening is one of those things that comes back pretty quickly once you make the decision to do it.

In fact, making the decision is the first and most critical step in designing your midlife marriage. The "empty nest" can be one of the most enjoyable and satisfying periods of your marriage, if you decide to make it so. Your primary work as parents is done and you can redirect your energies to yourselves and each other. Your relationship is deeper and more complex than it was when you were first married or when you were young parents, because your personalities have grown and deepened from your life experience. Chances are you don't know each other as well as you thought you did when the children were growing up, but that doesn't have to be a bad thing. In fact, it can be exciting, getting to know all the hidden facets of this remarkable individual sharing your life. The chicks may have flown, but there are plenty of feathers still to be gathered to decorate this new phase.

1. Renew your courtship, basing it this time on your shared history.
2. Take an interest in each other's activities, but don't take over.
3. Get in on the activity more often than you stand on sidelines.
4. Balance stubbornness with flexibility; be strong enough to bend.
5. Help each other figure out fire escapes for changes.
6. Listen to each other.

CHAPTER 13

Into the Sunset, Hand in Hand

These are not your grandparents' golden years. Sixty is no longer "old;" in fact, to a growing number of us, "old" doesn't really kick in until eighty-five or ninety, if then. Better sanitation practices, dramatic drops in infant mortality, and advances in medical care have shifted the average life expectancy from a mere forty-seven years for a child born in 1900 to seventy-seven years for a child born in 2000. Fewer of us are dying early of heart disease, cancer, and stroke. On the other hand, more of us are living long enough to develop chronic health problems like diabetes and dementia.

Between the physical changes we experience as we age and the enduring and pervasive negative stereotypes about old age, your own approaching "golden years" can feel less like a reward for a lifetime of hard work and more like being trapped on a pre-Columbian bridge over a raging river of lava, with dragons blocking the exit at one end and hippogryphs at the other. But once you know what some of the biggest roadblocks might be, you can plan a route that takes full advantage of all the richness and adventure this stage of life has to offer.

. . . .

Older People Are Happier

It's not surprising, given our propensity for glorifying youth, that younger Americans expect to be unhappier when they're older. But a recent survey on social trends by the Pew Research Center shows that older Americans are, in fact, happier than their younger counterparts. According to the study, the happiest people by age and gender are men age 65 and older, who are fifteen points happier than men between the ages of 18 and 29. Older women also are happier than younger women, although the "happiness gap" between younger and older women isn't as dramatic as it is for men.

I Love You; Now Go Away

For years, decades maybe, you and your spouse have commiserated over how much the obligations of your daily lives—careers, children, housework, social commitments—interfered with your ability to find time to enjoy each other as a couple. You squeezed in weekend getaways and the occasional dinner-for-two and dreamed of the day when you could do these things on a moment's notice, when your entire day would be yours to do with as you would. And now that day has arrived. The children are grown, you've officially retired, and your time is your own.

Chances are you've got a lot of time in front of you, too. While your grandparents might have looked forward to five, maybe ten years together in retirement, Baby Boomers and subsequent generations can reasonably expect to spend another fifteen, twenty, even thirty years together after they're old enough to start collecting Social Security or taking money out of their 401k)s.

That's a whole lot of togetherness. And, let's face it, as much as you love your spouse, you can get pretty darned sick of tripping over him or her everywhere you turn every moment of the day. As the old joke goes, you married each other for better or for worse, but not for breakfast, lunch, and dinner. In this new stage of your life, when the two of you have shared so much and know each other so well, it is perhaps more important than ever that you find ways to keep your relationship fresh and fulfilling. That means doing the same things you've done throughout your marriage: encouraging each other to explore individual interests, appreciating the opportunities to learn more about each other, and taking the time to enjoy activities together.

Do What Matters to You

One of the potential pitfalls of retirement is the loss of identity, which, for many of us, is wrapped up in our families and careers. Although we'll always be parents, the dynamics and demands of our relationships with our children change as they (and we) grow older; even though we've raised them to be independent adults, it can be a little alarming to realize that they no longer rely on you the same way they did when they were six or sixteen.

In a similar way, it can be a bit of a jolt to realize that, now that we no longer have to respond to the alarm clock five days a week, we sort of miss the office—the sense of being part of a team, of having our fingers on the company's pulse, of making a daily contribution and being valued for it. It can be kind of like withdrawal from an addictive drug, leaving us with a sense of emptiness or lack of purpose, even depression.

So what's the antidote?

First, you might have to challenge the way you think of retirement. If the word conjures up negative images for you (and it does for lots of people), rename this period of your life. Call it "the next chapter," for instance, or "second life," or even something goofy like "pre-geezerhood." Contrary to Shakespeare's notion that *a rose by any other name is still a rose*, changing the label for this phase can do much to change your expectations of what it can and ought to be. That keeps you from getting stuck in conventional "rules" for retirement and frees you to make it uniquely yours.

In fact, various studies and surveys have shown that people who take advantage of retirement to pursue a lifelong hobby or volunteer in a cause that excites them or start their own business or go back to school are happier, healthier, and longer-lived than those who view their retirement dinner as a putting-out-to-pasture ceremony.

There Are Benefits to Age

In a finding that won't surprise anyone over the age of sixty, a study of airline pilots showed that experience and training can more than compensate for decreased physical and mental skills associated with aging. In flight simulator testing conducted over three years with pilots between the ages of forty and sixty-nine, researchers found that the older pilots who had more training and experience scored better initially than their younger counterparts, and, although their skills did decline over the course of the study, the decline was not as great as it was for the younger pilots. Other studies have shown that specific skills requiring expertise—like typing or playing an instrument—tend to stay with people as they age, even as other skills grow weaker.

It might be hard for you and your spouse to figure out what you want your retirement to look like, so it's helpful to talk to each other about your goals, dreams, and fears. Once you know where each of you is coming from, you can figure out together how to proceed to where you want to be. Here are some questions to help you start the discussion:

- Do you want to stay in your community, or do you want to move to a different house or community or climate? What are the pros and cons of staying and of moving?
- How will you divide the household chores now that neither of you is working? Is the current division fair?
- Which social or civic commitments do you want to continue? Are there any you don't want to continue?
- What social or civic activities would you like to get involved with now that you have more time? Will those activities take more time than you'd like?
- What recreational activities would you like to pursue?
- If you hadn't ended up in the kind of work you were in, what field would you have liked to be in? Is it realistic to explore that field now?
- Finish this sentence: "Someday I'd like to . . ." Is "someday" in retirement? If not, why not?

Filling New Roles

One of the cool things about aging is that we continually get to try out new roles and grow into them over time. We've been friends and lovers and spouses and parents and employees and colleagues and a whole raft of other roles over the course of our adult lives. Now that we're eligible for senior citizen discounts, we have a new set of roles open to us: grandparent, mentor, sage, to name but three.

A great advantage to these new roles is that they give us a chance to see our spouses in a different light. After a lifetime of living with each other, it's easy to think we know each other inside and out, that all the nooks and crannies of our personalities have been charted, and that there is nothing new to discover. But the first time you see your spouse reading *Good Night Moon* to your grandchild, or helping a teenager learn to do woodworking, or showing someone how to use the new voting machines, you get a new glimpse into his or her internal make-up. Even if it just reminds you of something you already knew but had half-forgotten, the freshness imbues your relationship with its own vitality.

This is one important reason to do what you can to encourage your spouse to take on new tasks and challenges. Another key reason is your partner's mental health. Self-confidence, self-esteem, curiosity, and all the other "soft" qualities that keep our minds vigorous and healthy atrophy with lack of exercise the same way muscles do. Staying involved in the world through a hobby, a second career, volunteerism, or anything else that stimulates our minds and imaginations keeps us connected and interested, and that in turn helps keep us in shape physically.

Date Night, or Morning, or Afternoon

When there's so much time at your disposal, it's easy to slide on your commitment to dating your spouse. But it's still important to get out of the house and do things together; it might even be more important in retirement, just because you do have more time at home together. Getting out of the house gets you away from the niggling little things that irritate you at home and lets you concentrate on enjoying each other in a different setting.

One great advantage is that now you can make a date any time, assuming you don't let your schedules get too full with the things you've chosen to do in your post-career life. It can happen, almost without you realizing it, the same way it can happen almost accidentally at any other stage of your life. Renewing your commitment to dating ensures that you're still putting each other first, regardless of what other endeavors you may pursue.

Look at It This Way

Since at least the early 1900s, mystics and New Age enthusiasts have touted the idea that positive thinking can channel the energy of the universe to bring about positive changes in virtually every aspect of your life. But it's only recently that more empirical evidence has shown that there really are benefits to thinking good thoughts. A nine-year Dutch study showed that optimists were less likely to die from things like heart attacks and strokes than pessimists, and, in fact, optimists are less likely to die as early as pessimists from any cause. A Yale University study indicates that optimists live seven and a half years longer than pessimists. Other research shows that chronic stress—even the belief that you're under chronic stress—causes cells in your body to age faster, potentially cutting as much as a decade off your life.

· ·

You Really Are Only as Old as You Think

Several studies show that perceptions of old age really do have significant effects on older people's performance of routine tasks. A psychology professor at North Carolina State University showed that older people did better on memory tests if they were first told that age has little impact on memory; on the other hand, those who were prompted with old-age stereotypes did worse on the tests. And the Ohio Longitudinal Study of Aging and Retirement, a twenty-year study of people aged fifty and older who did not suffer from dementia, found that people who had positive ideas about aging lived an average of more than seven and a half years longer than people who saw aging as a negative thing. The difference in longevity remained even after researchers adjusted for variables like overall health, age, gender, and economic status.

Unfortunately, depression often becomes a problem as we get older. Sometimes it has been with us all along, but we didn't have time to recognize it until after retirement because we were too busy with work and family. Sometimes it starts late in life, and its causes can range from unmet expectations about our lives to chronic illness or other health issues. Typically, depression comes from hiding our feelings from ourselves as well as from others. But it can't be ignored forever, and it finds its outlet in one of four ways: hopelessness, temper, sadness, and anxiety.

"I Can't Do This Any More"

Hopelessness is a form of pessimism, in which you see the glass as half-empty. As you get older, this may take the form of thinking that your life is almost over instead of focusing on making the most of your opportunities. But it isn't really a lack of hope, as the word itself suggests; rather, the feeling it induces is the result of hiding your hopes. Many of us begin doing this as children in response to the common disappointments of childhood. If our hopes were dashed often enough as children, we connected hope to disappointment, and to avoid being disappointed, we learned to hide our hopes. As adults, we adopt the bromide, "Hope for the best and expect the worst," as protection against both getting our hopes up too high and getting bitterly disappointed. Children of alcoholics are particularly vulnerable to this form of depression as adults, because the alcoholic parent often made promises to the child but rarely kept those promises.

Train yourself for optimism

Researchers disagree over whether we can make ourselves more optimistic or not, and certainly pessimism is a challenging tendency to overcome. But there are some tricks you can use to focus your mind on the good things in your life and keep it from brooding on the negative.

- **Count your blessings.** Before you go to sleep each night, think of three good things that happened during the day. People who use this technique report feeling more satisfied and cheerful in their daily lives, and many find that, after a week or so, they're identifying many good things at the end of each day.
- **Keep a gratitude journal.** Writing down the things you've enjoyed or been grateful for in your life helps you zoom in on what's most valuable to you, and you may be surprised at how many good things you have to list.
- **Choose to hope.** Instead of looking for all the ways things can go wrong, try looking at the ways positive outcomes might be achieved. If you're accustomed to expecting rainy, cold weather the weekend that you plan to go hiking, for example, instead think how cozy and comforting it will be to sit in front of the fire with your spouse on a rainy, cold afternoon.

The Flare-Up

Losing your temper over trivial matters—what we call "flying off the handle"—can signal depression rooted in unexpressed anger. Like many emotional issues, this usually stems from experiences in childhood when we learned it was not acceptable to show our anger. We might have been punished or ignored, or someone (usually an adult) might have tried to make us feel guilty about being angry. So we learned to hide our anger. Not to *not be angry*, mind you, but to hide it from others. To hide it well, we had to hide it from ourselves, too. We got into the habit of denying we were angry, instead labeling our feelings as other things—hurt or disappointment, for instance.

This pattern gets reinforced in adulthood, too. Anger, though a natural response to injustice (real or perceived), is not socially acceptable—not in the workplace, not behind the steering wheel (think of the laws in your state against road rage or aggressive driving), and especially not in our relationships. So we continue to hide our anger as best we can.

But it comes out around the edges, so to speak, like a simmering pot suddenly boiling over. We blow up at trivial annoyances with a fury out of all proportion to the actual trigger. Worse, when it's appropriate for us to get angry, we can't; our lifelong habit of hiding our anger means that, when we should get angry over an injustice, we instead have a delayed reaction, and our anger is not only late but usually misdirected.

Here's something to remember about anger: It isn't necessarily a bad thing. When it comes in response to injustice and is directed properly, anger serves to energize us and strengthen our resolve to correct the injustice. It releases adrenaline so we can overcome our fears, and it helps our minds find solutions. Anger in this kind of situation is constructive. It's only the hidden anger, the kind that bursts out at unexpected and unwarranted times, that is destructive.

Decide to forgive

Self-talk can help you (or your partner) overcome the effects of hidden anger. Do an inventory of all the times you can remember when you were angry but weren't able to express your anger. It might be anything from a sibling breaking one of your toys, to finding out a romantic partner had lied to you, to getting an unfair dressing-down from your boss. As you picture each incident, say to yourself, "I want to forgive that person." Then move on to the next incident.

Note the phrasing of the self-talk here. The key isn't in forgiving; it's in making the decision to forgive. Telling yourself,

"I forgive that person," even if you don't really want to, might make you feel like a martyr, but it won't dissolve your hidden anger.

If your partner is suffering the effects of hidden anger, do not say, "I want you to forgive that person." This will set up resistance and could make the problem worse. Instead, if your spouse needs help getting started, say, "It's OK for you to forgive that person." This phrasing gives your spouse permission to let go of his or her anger, but it keeps the decision in his or her hands.

Lingering Grief

We aren't very good, as a society, at dealing with grief or sadness. From the moment we're born, everyone around us either wants to keep us from crying or to get us to stop crying as soon as possible. Skinned knees, hurt feelings, lost pets, broken toys, or overstrained nerves—the cause didn't matter as much as stanching the flow of tears did. We were told to stop crying long before we stopped feeling sad, and in order to stop crying, we had to learn to hide our sadness from ourselves.

In adulthood, crying is even less acceptable; think of Tom Hanks' line in *A League of Their Own*: "There's no crying in baseball!" There's also no crying in the office (it's not "professional"), no crying in front of the children (lest you make them feel sad), no crying in response to a physical injury ("Suck it up!"), and only limited crying in response to the death of a loved one. In many circumstances, it isn't even enough not to cry; if you betray any sign of sadness, your friends, family, and coworkers will urge you to "cheer up."

But hidden sadness, like hidden anger, will bubble out around the edges. You might cry over a sentimental television commercial, or over a stain on a favorite shirt, or over nothing at all. And yet you may find yourself unable to cry when it's appropriate, such as on hearing of the death of a friend.

Comforting yourself

You can bring about your own healing with the aid of a little imagination. You can go back in your mind to comfort the child you were when your puppy died, for instance. You can give the child-you sympathy, understanding, and a hug, and your subconscious mind will incorporate that new "experience" to support a healthy expression of sadness from now on. It might be hard for you to do this, because most of us have been told all our lives not to feel sorry for ourselves. But we can't comfort ourselves if we don't feel sorry for ourselves. And if we don't comfort ourselves, we will continue to battle hidden sadness.

You might worry, too, that you won't be able to stop crying once you start. If you've been hiding your sadness, fighting it, then it certainly can seem overwhelming and unending. But by comforting yourself, you're actually working through the grief, and when you're done, the sadness will be gone. If necessary, you can even make an appointment with yourself to do your grief work. Set aside half an hour when you can be sad in private; grieve on purpose, and use the full thirty minutes to think of all the things that have made you sad. If you feel overcome by sadness at inappropriate times, remind yourself of your "grief appointment"; this allows you to put aside your grief so it doesn't interfere with other activities.

Fear in Hiding

Children are continually told they aren't supposed to be scared. Adults tell them there's nothing to be afraid of; siblings and playmates make fun of them when they are afraid. But being told not to be afraid doesn't turn off fear, and being ridiculed for being afraid doesn't prompt us to be brave; we simply learn to hide our fear. If we get really good at hiding it, we even conceal it from ourselves.

Oh, sure, we might get a little overanxious about some things, and our spouses might think that worrying has become our new hobby. And these same spouses might get frustrated because they can't argue, comfort, or threaten us out of our anxiety; it's just too deep-seated. Because, when it comes right down to it, what we're afraid of is not being safe. It's very much like when we were little and afraid of the dark. Our fears were calmed if our parents turned on the light, showed us that there were no monsters lurking under the bed or in the closet, and then turned the light off again. But if we were simply told to quit stalling and go to sleep, maybe even threatened with punishment for voicing our fears, we learned to be afraid of fear itself, because the very act of being afraid made the whole situation worse.

It's hard to be safe

There are hazards at every stage of life. Children fear adults being angry with them; at school, they fear bullies, failing their classes, and being rejected socially. As we age, many of our fears center on our health. Denying or hiding these fears can lead us to neglect our health, and then our anxieties can become self-fulfilling prophecies. Acknowledging these fears, though, can prompt us to get regular medical check-ups, make healthy choices in our diets, and start a reasonable exercise regimen. And when spouses share their own and acknowledge each other's fears, they can work together to ensure their mutual well-being—encouraging each other to take the appropriate action and supporting each other in their choices.

Acknowledging fear also gives you the freedom to enjoy it. And we do enjoy fear; it's one of the key ingredients in excitement, and one of the elements that keeps life from being boring. You don't always have to let on to others that you're scared, but giving yourself permission to be afraid lets you choose when to share your fears and when to keep them to yourself.

. . . .

Alzheimer's Rises as Lifespan Increases

According to a report by the Alzheimer's Association, the rate of the disease is increasing as Americans enjoy longer lives; age, researchers say, is the main risk factor for developing this most common and ultimately fatal form of dementia. The disease strikes about one in eight people over age sixty-five and nearly four in ten people over age eighty-five. More than five million Americans suffer from Alzheimer's, and that number is expected to triple by 2050 as the eighty-five-plus population swells with long-lived Baby Boomers.

Taking Care of Yourself and Each Other

As Bette Davis observed, "Old age is not for sissies." The hazards are many and varied. Being overweight or obese not only strains your cardiovascular system and heightens your risk for chronic illnesses like diabetes, it also puts additional stress on your joints and can lead to or exacerbate the pain and lack of mobility associated with osteoarthritis. As you age, you are likely to have more trouble seeing in the dark and it will take your eyes longer to adjust from bright conditions to dim ones, and vice versa; you also are likely to develop cataracts and may need surgery to remove them. Medications may interfere with your enjoyment of sex. And if all that weren't enough to worry about, the longer you live, the higher your risk of developing some form of physical or mental frailty. In fact, "frailty" is a medical condition in its own right, and it strikes about 25 percent of people between the ages of eighty-five and eighty-nine, compared with only 10 percent of those in their mid-to-late seventies.

But aging is one of the many areas where married couples fare better than single people. No one is exactly sure why, but researchers believe that married couples provide essential support for each other when it comes to watching your diet, exercising regularly, getting regular medical care, taking prescriptions properly, and maintaining an interest in life.

. . . .

Sex and Seniors

A University of Florida analysis of data from the National Survey of Families and Households showed that more than half of married couples aged sixty and older have sex at least once a month, and most engage in sex once a week. The rate dropped to about one in four when the couples were seventy-six or older, and the frequency of sexual activity was lower when one or both partner's health was poor. Self-esteem and self-image also affect interest in sex as we age, so ensuring your partner knows you find him or her desirable is an integral part of keeping physical intimacy in your relationship.

No matter how old you and your partner are now, there are several things you can do to improve your health today and continue reaping the benefits tomorrow:

- **Add more fruits, vegetables, and lean meat to your diet.** Antioxidants and other nutrients in fruits and vegetables help ward off heart disease and keep cholesterol at desirable levels, while lean meats give you essential protein without so much of the artery-clogging animal fats.
- **Walk, swim, bicycle, and lift—according to your doctor's recommendations.** A varied exercise routine helps tone muscles and keeps your cardiovascular system functioning properly. Loss of muscle mass can make conditions like arthritis even more debilitating.
- **Follow the directions on your prescription medications.** Ask your doctor or pharmacist about side effects and

how your medications interact with each other. Find out whether over-the-counter pain killers, vitamins, or herbal supplements will interfere with your medications.

- **Get regular eye and dental check-ups.** Eye exams can detect potentially serious problems like macular degeneration or glaucoma, while gum disease has been linked to heart problems.

- **"Age-proof" your home.** Plug in night-lights in bathrooms, bedrooms, and hallways to make it easier to navigate at night. Keep walkways and stairs clear of clutter, and remove area rugs that might slip underneath your feet. If necessary, install grab bars in tubs and showers and next to toilets.

- **Exercise your brain.** Activities like solving crosswords and playing cards help keep your mind nimble. Check out Web sites like *www.HappyNeuron.com* and *www.MyBrainTrainer.com* for "brain calisthenics," or invest in a video game system; some, like Nintendo's Wii, gently exercise your body as well as your mind.

Many couples experience a bit of friction when they first leave their jobs and learn to be around each other during more hours of the day. As with any other phase in your marriage, you have to be willing to listen to each other, respect each other's point of view, and work together to find solutions to issues that crop up. If you continue to value and maintain your marriage throughout the years, you'll keep the bond between you supple, flexible, and strong. It might take a little time to get used to your new lifestyle, but once you make the adjustment, these really can become your golden years.

1. Talk to each other about your goals, dreams, and visions of retirement.
2. Find a passion that sustains your interest and sense of self, and encourage your spouse to do the same.
3. Renew your commitment to dating, especially away from home.
4. Encourage each other to eat healthfully, follow doctor's instructions, and stay physically and mentally active.
5. Help each other deal with issues that might lead to depression; if necessary, provide support and encouragement for seeking professional help.

CHAPTER 14

Smoothing the Rough Edges

There is bound to be a certain amount of friction in any marriage. Some of it will be serious, requiring a concerted effort and willingness to work things out to resolve. But most of it will be trivial—the tiny, day-to-day irritations that sometimes make us want to tear at our hair and scream into the wilderness. Like every other aspect of your marriage, you can view friction as a problem or as a challenge. When it's a challenge, you can meet it together.

There's another way to view friction: as a process of polishing. It's similar to the way sea glass is created. When pieces of glass are tossed overboard from ships into the ocean, they are tossed and tumbled with the waves and the sand until the sharp edges are worn down and the surface is polished to a smooth, high sheen. By the time it washes ashore, sea glass looks like a priceless gem— a diamond, an emerald, a sapphire, or a piece of rare amber. You and your spouse act on each other like the water and the sand on the sea glass, rubbing away at the sharp edges of your personalities and allowing the gems within to come into full view.

Indeed, the very nature of marriage represents a lifelong growth opportunity for both of you, helping each of you, in ways you might never fully recognize, to deal with a variety of issues that are common to many of us.

Common Rough Edges

Each person is unique, and each of us has a unique combination of sharp edges, shaped by our personalities, our experiences, and our expectations for the future. But there are some common areas that can create the friction necessary to polish each other to a sparkling finish.

A Place for Everything . . .

Maybe you're the kind of person who has to be organized in everything. You have a specific place for everything in your home, and you feel like ants are crawling all over you when something isn't in its proper place. Your life is one big collection of lists—to-do lists, shopping lists, lists of people to call, bills to pay, e-mail to answer, and so on. If you go to bed without folding that last load of laundry, you don't sleep well. You cannot function without a watch and a calendar. For you, life has to be predictable and well-ordered. You don't like discomfort, surprises, or last-minute changes. Chaos makes you cranky.

You expect your partner to feel the same way you do about these things. But your spouse might not be like you. Maybe she can tolerate a bit of clutter around the house, and maybe she actually enjoys an unexpected interruption in her day. Maybe she gets these crazy ideas for doing things on the spur of the moment, like going to see a movie tonight when you had planned to sit in your favorite armchair and catch up on some reading. You just don't get her attitude, and the only solution that makes sense to you is to try to organize her, too.

She'll probably resist your attempts to organize her, and you'll probably both experience some frustration before you reach a workable compromise. In the end, though, you'll end up being a little less rigid and more accepting of the chaos that you cannot control, maybe even learning to enjoy it occasionally, and she'll learn the benefits of being a little more organized. Both of you will grow, in complementary ways.

What Will the Neighbors Think?

Maybe you're painfully aware of the opinions of others; you want people to think well of you, and you're mortified if you think you might have offended someone. You want to impress everyone, and you want your partner to impress them, too; after all, his accomplishments reflect on you as well. You don't like to confront others, and you don't want him to get involved in confrontations, either. It is absolutely essential that both of you put your best face forward to the world, avoiding any word or gesture that might lead others to form a poor opinion of you, even if only temporarily.

It's unlikely that your spouse is as concerned about what other people think as you are. He might feel free to say anything to anyone at any time, as long as it's honest or done for a laugh. He might not care whether he offends someone, or whether that person will respect or admire him. The foibles that embarrass you are funny little quirks to him, and if you get upset at his revealing your quirks to others, he may be astonished that you don't see the humor. The more you try to get him to consider the opinions of others, the more he tries to get you to ignore them.

In the course of this struggle, you learn that people can know unimpressive things about you and like you anyway. You may find that expressing your own opinion leads others to respect you more than they would if you just went along with their opinions. And your spouse learns to identify the fine line between sharing common human foibles and making someone feel ridiculed, and perhaps he learns to temper his outspokenness with consideration for others' feelings. Each of you brings the other to a happier middle ground.

Not Good Enough

Maybe you're something of a perfectionist. You pay attention to detail. You read the fine print before signing anything; you look for flaws and usually succeed at finding them, even if they're minor; you train yourself to do things right and counsel others on how to do better. You feel terrible if you make a mistake, and your bad feelings can be out of all proportion to the magnitude of the error. When others make mistakes, you can get angry, especially if you feel you've been duped or taken advantage of. Others might think you're something of a pessimist, because you're always on the lookout for pitfalls.

Your spouse probably is not so concerned with details or getting things right. She may take things as they come, assume the fine print is OK and doesn't need to be read, and be blind to small flaws like a new ding in the car door or the fact that the picture over the fireplace tilts ever so slightly to the left. Maybe she makes decisions based on her mood at the time, and she resists your attempts to make her confront problems logically.

As your styles come up against each other day after day, you learn to focus your perfectionist tendencies on the things that are most important to you and to be content with "good enough" in other areas. You use your logic to temper your pessimism, accepting that not every potential pitfall is likely to crop up. Meanwhile, your spouse learns to pay attention to details when it matters and to combine emotion and logic when it comes to making important decisions. Each of you learns to use your strengths to complement the other's.

Footloose and Fancy Free

Maybe you're the creative, spontaneous type, always coming up with grand ideas and making fabulous leaps of logic. You don't worry about details and are unequivocally optimistic, assuming that problems will work themselves out. Details bore you, and you tend to get impatient with slowness in any area of life. You might cut corners and take risks that scare your spouse. You may feel an unusually high sense of obligation to friends and family and often put their needs before your own or those of your spouse.

Your spouse probably is not quite as freewheeling as you are. She might try to rein you in a little, and she may get angry when you pooh-pooh her fears. You might have frequent arguments about money, because she wants to save for the future and you want to live for the moment. The more you try to encourage her to enjoy the here and now, the more she worries about tomorrow.

As you butt heads over your differing philosophies, you learn to control your impulses and balance them against what you want for the future, and she learns to enjoy giving in to the occasional wild urge. She becomes more flexible, and you become more deliberate. Both of you have more fun, because you have learned how to mesh each other's styles.

My Way or the Highway

Maybe you feel you need to be in control. If your childhood was chaotic—if you had to submit to the whims of older siblings and were unable to make your own choices—you might have grown up thinking you aren't going to ever let anyone control you again. In your marriage, you might insist on making all the decisions. Maybe you control the finances; maybe you even hide money from your spouse. You make the rules and expect your spouse to follow them; you insist on knowing everything about your spouse's activities and may even refuse to let your spouse do things on his or her own. You've learned that anger is a useful tool because most people are afraid of anger, so when you feel your control slipping, you use anger to restore it.

Your spouse probably doesn't want to be controlled. He wants to do his own thing, within the boundaries of your relationship but without asking your permission or seeking your approval. He wants to be able to disagree with you and to have a voice in making decisions that affect both of you. He wants you to respect him as a full partner in your relationship.

This kind of friction can help you learn to regard your spouse as an adult, capable of making his own decisions and sharing in the responsibilities of your relationship. Your spouse can become more attuned to your feelings, making an effort to invite your participation rather than taking it for granted. You help each other move toward a relationship of equals and foster the interdependence that affirms your bond.

No matter what incarnation your own rough edges assume, it takes a lifetime of gentle friction to smooth them down. Of course, to polish each other, you and your spouse have to start from a foundation of equality, trust, commitment, and communication. The couple who supports each other without either overburdening the other, who is secure in the relationship, who is dedicated to building a good life together, and who can talk openly without getting or making each other angry—this is the couple who, even though they get on each other's nerves once in a while, will rub each other the right way in the long term, providing the support that lets each partner grow freely and flourish for a lifetime.

APPENDIX A

Staying Safe

According to statistics from the U.S. Justice Department, married people are significantly less likely to be victims of domestic violence or any type of violent crime—from simple assault to homicide—than single or divorced people. Men and women who were separated or divorced reported the highest rates of what researchers call "nonfatal intimate partner violence," while those who were married or widowed had the lowest rates, according to the Justice Department's Bureau of Justice Statistics.

Why this should be so is less clear. Some experts believe that married people are more invested in their spouses' well-being and therefore are less likely to resort to hitting, punching, kicking, and other forms of violence. Your risk also depends on more than your marital status. The younger, poorer, and less educated you are, the more likely you are to be victimized by an intimate partner.

But even with greater awareness, education, and resources for dealing with domestic violence, nearly one in four women and about eight in one hundred men will be victimized by a violent partner at some point. Although men can be physically and emotionally battered by women (and may be less likely to report it or seek help), women are still much more likely to be the victims of domestic violence.

What Constitutes Abuse?

For the great majority of us, occasional arguments will be the worst conflict we endure in our marriages. But sometimes those arguments escalate into something more, and sometimes we're simply afraid that they will but we don't know what to look for. The question of what constitutes abuse is a complex one, because there are so many ways of exerting power and control—the objective of all abuse, whether it's physical, emotional, verbal, or sexual. Usually, an abuser uses several tactics to intimidate his partner, and some of them may be less obvious than others.

Physical Abuse

This is what comes to mind most readily when we hear the term *domestic violence*. Physical abuse includes all the things we normally think of: pushing, punching, slapping, kicking, biting, burning, arm-twisting, and so on. It may involve weapons; often, it's bare-knuckle. Less common tactics, but ones that also put the victim at risk of physical harm, include driving recklessly, locking the victim out of the house, withholding food, or leaving the victim in a dangerous place.

Verbal and Emotional Abuse

Sometimes referred to as psychological abuse, this behavior consists of isolating and belittling the victim. The abuser might routinely insult, ridicule, or humiliate his victim. He might cut off his victim's access to friends and family by not allowing her to use the telephone or the computer, for instance. He might use more subtle means, too, like trying to make her feel guilty about spending time away from him, or issuing a "them or me" ultimatum. He may discourage her from holding a job, or, if she does work, he may call or visit so frequently that she is unable to keep the job. He may threaten suicide if she tries to leave him, or he may threaten to kill her. He may insist on controlling the money so she has no means to leave.

. . . .

Where to Get Help

In the middle of an attack, or when an attack seems likely, call 911. If you are not in immediate physical danger, call the National Domestic Violence Hotline (www.ndvh.org) at 1-800-799-SAFE (7233) or 1-800-787-3224 (TTY service for the hearing impaired). You also can ask your physician or health care provider for a referral to a counselor or shelter, or your church also may be able to direct you to local organizations dedicated to helping victims of abuse.

Leaving is usually psychologically difficult for the victim, too. Most victims know they are at greatest risk of serious physical injury or death at the point of departure. The abusive partner may also engage in other forms of abuse after the victim leaves, like stalking her or "parental abduction"—kidnapping the children. One study found that the average abused woman leaves her abuser and returns seven times before she finally gets out of the relationship permanently.

Sexual Abuse

Sometimes an abuser will use sex as his primary tool for controlling his partner. He may insult her physical attributes or sexual performance, often in front of others as a way of humiliating her. He may make demeaning jokes about women in general and treat his partner as a sex object. He may force sex on his partner or subject her to unwanted touching, either in public or in private. He may insist on sexual activities that make her feel degraded. Sexual abuse is often confusing to the victim, because sex is such an integral part of an intimate relationship. The key is in how sex with your partner makes you feel. If it makes you feel attractive, desirable, and loved, it isn't abusive. If it makes you feel objectified, used, or frightened, it very likely qualifies as abuse.

Abused Men

According to a study of men who went to emergency rooms for medical care, 13 percent reported being physically abused by a female partner in the preceding twelve months. Of those, half said they had been kicked, bitten, punched, or choked, and more than a third reported that the abuse incident involved a weapon. Seven percent said their female partners had forced them to have sex.

The Abuse Cycle

Abuse can take several different forms, but it almost always follows the same pattern: a period of calm, even loving behavior, followed by a build-up of tension and culminating in an explosion. If nothing changes, the cycle repeats itself endless times, although the duration of each phase may vary wildly from cycle to cycle. Most relationships start with the calm, loving phase, and it may last quite a long time, even up to the wedding day.

Sweethearts Still . . .

The calm, loving period usually marks the start of the relationship, but its reappearance after the explosion can be the most confusing time for victims. The attacker is remorseful and even panicky that the victim will leave or file charges. The victim, horrified at what has happened, tries desperately to reconcile the loving relationship she thought she had with the violence she just experienced, and, when she is unable to do so, prefers to believe in the attacker's remorse and his promises that it will never happen again.

It should be noted that the remorse is usually quite genuine, although it is seldom a deterrent to a repetition of the violence. And though the attacker may fully intend, at least at the time, never to hurt his partner again, the memory of that promise seldom stays his hand. The remorse and the promises come from the attacker's fear of being abandoned by his partner. The abuse continues, though, because other emotional problems are stronger than that fear.

When the victim accepts the attacker's apologies and promises, a new period of calm sets in. However, this "honeymoon" phase tends to be shorter each time the cycle of abuse repeats itself, and in time it may disappear altogether. Gradually, the tension begins to build again as the abuser becomes more irritable, more critical, and more accusatory, while the victim becomes more suppliant, trying to ward off another violent episode by appeasing her partner.

The Gathering Storm

As we discussed earlier, most of us don't like it when someone is angry with us because when adults got angry with us when we were kids, the anger felt threatening to us. Back then, we backed away from anger, waited it out, and were on our best behavior so we wouldn't incite another burst of anger. To this day, we still tend to back away, wait it out, and try to placate anyone who's angry with us.

This almost universal behavior makes anger a most effective tool for intimidating and controlling others. Bosses use it in the workplace, customers use it in the store, and spouses use it at home. And employees, store managers, and spouses do what the angry person wants because they've been trained all their lives to avoid confrontation.

In an abusive relationship, though, appeasement doesn't work. In fact, it has the opposite effect: The other's anger actually intensifies. The more you try to placate your spouse, the less rational your spouse becomes.

. . . .

Under the Influence

There's a popular misconception that husbands and wives get violent most often when they're under the influence of alcohol or drugs. In fact, according to Justice Department figures, alcohol plays a role in only about a third of instances of domestic violence against women and only 20 percent of attacks against men. Drug use is even less common in relation to domestic violence, with attackers reported as being under the influence of drugs in a mere 6 percent of instances.

The Explosion

Like a steaming teakettle about to whistle, the build-up of anger finally reaches a point where the only outlet for all that energy is a violent episode. The abusive spouse either cannot or is not willing to control his or her rage, so he or she takes it out on the passive spouse. The abuse might consist of actual physical violence or threats, or, more likely, a combination of the two. Afterwards, the attacker usually is calm because his or her anger has been released, and the victim is emotional, hurt and frightened by the attack.

For years, this dynamic confounded police responding to domestic abuse calls; when they arrived, they typically found a hysterical woman making wild accusations against her husband or boyfriend, who was often soft-spoken, rational, and cooperative. Since the federal Violence Against Women Act took effect in the mid-1990s, however, police training and automatic arrest laws—which don't require the victim to press charges—have helped ensure that victims of abuse aren't re-victimized by the authorities they call for help.

APPENDIX B

References

AmeriStatstaff. "Marriage Boosts Individual Earnings," *www.prb.org/Articles/2003/MarriageBoostsIndividualEarnings.aspx*, March 2003. (accessed February 2007)

Associated Press. "Reality Check: 95 Percent of Americans Had Premarital Sex," *www.cnn.com*, 19 December 2006. (accessed December 2006)

————. "Sex Troubles Points to Health Issues," *www.msnbc.com*, 8 February 2007. (accessed February 2007)

————. "Sexy People Play the Symmetry Card," *www.msnbc.com*, 9 January 2007. (accessed January 2007)

Atkins, D. C., D. H. Baucom, and N. S. Jacobson. "Understanding Infidelity: Correlates in a National Random Sample," *Journal of Family Psychology* 15, no. 4 (2001): 735–49.

Bailey, D. Smith. "Compulsive Cybersex Can Jeopardize Marriage, Rest of Life," *Monitor on Psychology* 32, no. 9 (October 2003): 20.

Bayou, Bradley. *Science of Sexy: Dress to Fit Your Unique Figure with the Style System That Works for Every Shape and Size.* New York: Gotham, 2006.

Belluck, Pam. "As Minds Age, What's Next? Brain Calisthenics," *New York Times*, 27 December 2006.

Britt, Robert Roy. "Fear Could Be Linked to Cancer," *www.livescience.com*, 19 October 2006. (accessed February 2007)

Brody, Jane E. "The Importance of Knowing What the Doctor Is Talking About," *New York Times*, 30 January 2007.

Carey, Benedict. "For Couples, Reaction to Good News Matters More than Reaction to Bad," *New York Times*, 5 December 2006.

————. "Insufferable Clinginess, or Healthy Dependence?" *New York Times*, 6 March 2007.

————. "Just Thinking about Money Can Turn the Mind Stingy," *New York Times*, 21 November 2006.

Carmichael, Mary. "Can Exercise Make You Smarter?" *Newsweek*, 26 March 2007.

Catalano, Shannan. "Intimate Partner Violence in the United States." *www.ojp.usdoj.gov/bjs/intimate/ipv.htm*, 28 December 2006. (accessed March 2007)

Chethik, Neil. *Voicemale: What Husbands Really Think about Their Marriages, Their Wives, Sex, Housework and Commitment.* New York: Simon & Schuster, 2006.

Christopher, F. Scott, and Susan Sprecher. "Sexuality in Marriage, Dating, and Other Relationships: A Decade Review," *Journal of Marriage and Family* 62, no. 4 (November 2000): 999–1017.

Darlin, Damon. "Extra Weight, Higher Costs," *New York Times*, 2 December 2006.

Davis, Jeanie Lerche. "Close Relationship Helps Heart: Conversations with Close Friend Offset Risk of Death after Heart Attack," *WebMD Medical News*, *www.webmd.com*, 14 April 2004. (accessed January 2007)

Dingfelder, S. "Men Who Cheat Show Elevated Testosterone Levels," *Monitor on Psychology* 37, no. 11 (December 2006): 10.

Dobson, Roger. "Anti-Stress Benefits of Holding Hands," *The Independent*, 7 August 2005.

Donnelly, Denise A. "Sexually Inactive Marriages," *Journal of Sex Research* 30, no. 2 (1993): 171–79.

Forbes.com. "Sex Does the Body Good," *www.msnbc.com*, 19 December 2006. (accessed January 2007)

Gable, S. L., G. Gonzaga, and A. Strachman. "Will You Be There for Me When Things Go Right? Social Support for Positive Events," *Journal of Personality and Social Psychology* 91 (2006): 904–17.

Giles, G. G., G. Severi, D. R. English, M. R. E. McCredie, R. Borland, P. Boyle, and J. L. Hopper. "Sexual Factors and Prostate Cancer," *British Journal of Urology International* 92, no. 3 (2003): 211.

Goldberg, Carole T. "Empty Nest and Full Heart as Children Leave Home," *Yale Health Care* 6, no. 5 (September-October 2003): 1.

Gorman, Elizabeth H. "The Effect of Marital Status on Attitudes Toward Pay and Finances," *Work and Occupations* 27, no. 1 (2000): 64–88.

HealthDay News. "Marriage Boosts Parents' Mental Health," 28 September 2006. *www.healthday.com/Article.asp?AID=535193* (accessed December 2006 via *www.forbes.com*)

Hughes, Chris. "42% of Young Men Fake Their Orgasms," *The Mirror* (London), 17 January 2005.

Huston, Ted L., and Anita L. Vangelisti. "Socioemotional Behavior and Satisfaction in Marital Relationships: A Longitudinal Study," *Journal of Personality and Social Psychology* 61, no. 5 (1991): 721–33.

Cooking Light magazine. "America's Healthy Living Habits: How Do You Compare?" Insight 2007 questionnaire. *www.cnn.com.* 26 January 2007. (accessed January 2007)

Johnsen, Jennifer, MPH. "Relationship Abuse, Intimate Partner Violence, and Domestic Violence Threatens Individuals and Society," Katharine Dexter McCormick Library, Planned Parenthood Federation of America, 1 June 2005. *http://www.plannedparenthood.org/news-articles-press/politics-policy-issues/medical-sexual-health/relationship-violence-6364.htm* (accessed April 2007)

Kadlec, Dan. "Reversal of Fortune: She Makes More than He," *Money*, 20 February 2007.

Kantrowitz, Barbara. "National Sleep Survey Finds Weary Women," *Newsweek* Web exclusive, *www.newsweek.com*, 7 March 2007. (accessed March 2007).

Kaplan, Robert M., and Richard G. Kronick. "Marital Status and Longevity in the United States Population," *Journal of Epidemiology and Community Health* 60 (2006): 760–65.

Keck, Kristi. "Emotional Changes of Retirement Can Tarnish Golden Years," *www.cnn.com*, 9 January 2007. (accessed February 2007)

Kiecolt-Glaser, Janice K., and Tamara L. Newton. "Marriage and Health: His and Hers," *Psychological Bulletin* 127, no. 4 (2001): 472–503.

Kposowa, Augustine J. "Marital Status and Suicide in the National Longitudinal Mortality Study," *Journal of Epidemiology and Community Health* 54 (2000): 254–61.

Lieberman, Matthew D., and Naomi Eisenberg. *Social Neuroscience: People Thinking about People.* Boston: M.I.T. Press, 2005.

Matthias, Ruth E., James E. Lubben, Kathryn A. Atchison, and Stuart O. Schweitzer. "Sexual Activity and Satisfaction among Very Old Adults: Results from a Community-Dwelling Medicare Population Survey," *The Gerontologist* 37, no. 1 (1997): 6–14.

Marsiglio, W., and D. Donnelly. "Sexual Relations in Later Life: a National Study of Married Persons," *Journal of Gerontology* (November 1991): 338–44.

Mayo Clinic Staff. "Healthy Marriage: Why Love Is Good for You," *www.mayoclinic.com*, 6 February 2006. (accessed December 2006)

Medical News Today. "People with Depression Benefit More from Marriage than Others," *www.medicalnewstoday.com*, 15 August 2006. (accessed January 2007)

Michael, Robert T., John H. Gagnon, Edward O. Laumann, and Gina Kolata. *Sex in America: A Definitive Survey.* Boston: Little, Brown, 1995.

Morokoff, Patricia J., and Gillilland, Ruth. "Stress, Sexual Functioning, and Marital Satisfaction," *Journal of Sex Research* 30 no. 1 (1993): 43–53.

Nagourney, Eric. "Financial Troubles Can Affect the Heart," *New York Times*, 20 March 2007.

Nagourney, Eric. "Test of Pilots Shows Age May Be Advantageous," *New York Times*, 6 March 2007.

National Center for Injury Prevention and Control. "Costs of Intimate Partner Violence Against Women in the United States." Atlanta, Georgia: Centers for Disease Control and Prevention. *www.cdc.gov/ncipc/pub-res/ipv_cost/IPVBook-Final-Feb18.pdf.* March 2003. (accessed March 2007)

Osborne, Cynthia, and McLanahan, Sara. "Partnership Instability and Child Well-Being," Center for Research on Child Well-being, Working Paper #2004-16-FF. October 2004. *http://crcw.princeton.edu/workingpapers/WP04-16-FF-Osborne.pdf.* (accessed February 2007)

Persaud, Raj. "Semen Acts as an Anti-Depressant," *New Scientist*, 26 June 2002, *www.newscientist.com.* (accessed January 2007)

Pew Research Center. "A Barometer of Modern Morals: Sex, Drugs and the 1040," *http://pewresearch.org/pubs/307/a-barometer-of-modern-morals*, 28 March 2006. (accessed January 2007)

Popenoe, David. "The Top Ten Myths of Marriage," *http://marriage.rutgers.edu/Publications/pubmyths%20of%20marriage.htm.* (accessed December 2006)

Priedt, Robert. "Domestic Abuse Costs 'Enormous' for Women: Study." HealthDay, *www.nlm.nih.gov/medlineplus/news/fullstory_44588.html*, 30 January 2007. (accessed April 2007)

Rabin, Roni. "It Seems the Fertility Clock Ticks for Men, Too," *New York Times*, 27 February 2007.

Rand Research Brief. "Health, Marriage, and Longer Life for Men." RB-5018, 1998, http://rand.org/pubs/research_briefs/RB5018/index1.html. (accessed December 2006)

Reuters. "Bad at Math? Worrying Makes Matters Worse," *www.msnbc.com*, 20 February 2007. (accessed March 2007)

Reuters. "Childhood Obesity Can Trigger Early Puberty," *www.msnbc.com*, 5 March 2007. (accessed March 2007)

Reuters. "Diet, Exercise Take Off Equal Pounds, Study Finds," *www.cnn.com*, 29 January 2007. (accessed January 2007)

Reuters. "Human Attraction on Second Thought," *www.cnn.com*, 18 January 2007. (accessed January 2007)

Reuters. "Kids Who Sleep More Weigh Less," *www.msnbc.com*, 7 February 2007. (accessed February 2007)

Reuters. "Loneliness Tied to Physical Ills," *www.msnbc.com*, 6 February 2007. (accessed February 2007)

Reuters. "Migraine Meds Could Treat Orgasmic Headaches," *www.msnbc.com*, 26 January 2007. (accessed January 2007)

Reuters. "Obese Couples Have Tough Time Having Babies," *www.msnbc.com*, 7 March 2007. (accessed March 2007)

Reuters. "Study Shows Why Exercise Boosts Brainpower," *www*
.cnn.com, 12 March 2007. (accessed March 2007)

Reuters Health. "Many Older Women Abused by Their Partner," *www.nlm.nih.gov/medlineplus/news/fullstory_46592.html*,
15 March 2007. (accessed March 2007)

Robinson, Marnia. "Why Does a Lover Pull Away after Sex?"
www.reuniting.info/science/dopamine_separation_after_orgasm,
23 June 2005. (accessed January 2007)

Selvin, Molly. "More Wives Becoming Main Breadwinners," *Los
Angeles Times*, as published on *www.chicagotribune.com*, 11 February 2007. (accessed February 2007)

Simon, Robin W. "Revisiting the Relationship among Gender,
Marital Status, and Mental Health," *American Journal of Sociology*
107, no. 4 (2002): 1065–96.

Smith, George Davey, Stephen Frankell, and John Yarnell. "Sex
and Death: Are They Related? Findings from the Caerphilly
Cohort Study," *British Medical Journal* 315 (1997): 1641–44.

Stam, Z. "Optimists Have Longer, More Satisfying Relationships,
Study Suggests," *Monitor on Psychology* 37, no. 8 (8 September
2006): 15.

St. George, Donna. "Moms' Time with Kids Rising," *Washington
Post*, as published on *www.msnbc.com*, 20 March 2007. (accessed
March 2007)

Thompson, Andrea. "Brain Can Learn Fear by Seeing Others'
Fears," *www.livescience.com*, 20 March 2007. (accessed March
2007)

Tierney, John. "The Voices in My Head Say 'Buy It!' Why Argue?" *New York Times*, 16 January 2007.

University of Maryland School of Medicine. "Study Shows Laughter Helps Blood Vessels Function Better," press release, 7 March 2005, *www.umm.edu/news/releases/laughter2.htm.* (accessed March 2007)

University of North Texas news service. "Sex among Married Ignored by Hollywood," press release, 27 October 2000, *http:// web2.unt.edu/news/story.cfm?story=7901.* (accessed January 2007)

Urbani, Diane. "Can Regular Sex Ward Off Colds and Flu?" *New Scientist*, 17 April 1999. *www.newscientist.com.* (accessed January 2007)

U.S. Department of Health and Human Services. "Healthy Marriage Initiative, Benefits of Healthy Marriages," *http://www.acf .hhs.gov/healthymarriage/benefits/index.html#children,* 27 November 2006. (accessed December 2006)

Van Dusen, Allison. "Boomers' Health Mistakes Can Add Up Later," *www.forbes.com* and *www.msnbc.com,* 19 January 2007. (accessed January 2007)

Wadyka, Sally. "Free the Mind and Fewer Injuries May Follow," *New York Times*, 4 January 2007.

Waite, Linda, and Gallagher, Maggie. *The Case for Marriage: Why Married People Are Happier, Healthier, and Better off Financially.* New York: Doubleday, 2000.

Wilcox, W. Bradford et al. *Why Marriage Matters: 26 Conclusions from the Social Sciences.* New York: Institute for American Values, 2002.

www.foreverfamilies.net. "Immunized Against Infidelity: 'Affair-proofing' Your Marriage," *www.foreverfamilies.net/xml/articles/immunized_infidelity.aspx?* (accessed March 2007)

www.foreverfamilies.net. "Increasing Intimacy in Marriage," *www.foreverfamilies.net/xml/articles/marital_intimacy.aspx?* (accessed March 2007)

Yara, Susan. "Fathers' Empty Nest," *www.forbes.com*, 23 August 2006.

INDEX